JOY OF LIVING BIBLE STUDY SERIES

WALKING IN GOD'S WAY

Studies in Ruth and Esther

Life-related for Personal and Group Study

RUTH BATHAUER & DORIS W. GREIG

GL
Regal Books
A Division of GL Publications
Ventura, California, U.S.A.

Published by Regal Books
A Division of GL Publications
Ventura, California 93006
Printed in U.S.A.

Cover photo by Stacey Martin.

Poems by Donna Pace. Used by permission.

Any omission of credits or permissions granted is unintentional. The publisher requests documentation for future printings.
Library of Congress Cataloging in Publication Data

Bathauer, Ruth M.
  Walking in God's way: studies in Ruth and Esther / by Ruth M. Bathauer and Doris W. Greig.
    p.   cm.
  ISBN 0-8307-1284-4
  1. Bible. O.T. Ruth—Criticism, interpretation, etc. 2. Bible O.T. Esther—Criticism, interpretation, etc. 3. Woman (Theology)—Biblical teaching. I. Greig, Doris W., 1926- . II. Title.
BS1315.2.B37   1988
222'.3506—dc19   88-2451
                                                                              CIP

1 2 3 4 5 6 7 8 9 10 / 91 90 89 88 87

Rights for publishing this book in other languages are contracted by Gospel Literature International (GLINT) foundation. GLINT also provides technical help for the adaptation, translation, and publishing of Bible study resources and books in scores of languages worldwide. For further information, contact GLINT, Post Office Box 488, Rosemead, California, 91770, U.S.A., or the publisher.

SPECIAL BENEFIT

This book has been conveniently hole-punched and perforated for easy tearout and insertion in a 6" × 9½" looseleaf notebook:

- Bible study pages lie flat in your notebook for ease of writing as you study.
- Additional notebook paper can be inserted for journaling or more extensive notes and other relevant information.
- Additional studies in the Joy of Living Series can be inserted, along with your personal notes, and tabbed to help you build your Bible study file for easy, future reference.

CONTENTS

Introduction   7

How to Use this Book   9

PART I   RUTH

1. A Tale of Love   13
*A lesson in self-sacrificing love
and unselfish commitment*

2. Love's Rich Dividends   29
*Learn about the wonderful message
of God's love for you!*

PART II   ESTHER

3. A Queen Is Dethroned   45
*God, by His providence, is leading
us every step of the way.*

4. A New Queen Is Chosen   63
*Unlikely circumstances never
stand in the way of God's perfect plan!*

5. For Such a Time as This   81
*Discouraged? God has you where you are
for a special reason.*

6. Our Perfect Strength and Shield   99
*You may be cast down,
but you are not destroyed!*

7. A Marvelous Deliverance   115
*God is still on the throne,
and He gives us the victory!*

INTRODUCTION

The Bible is full of stories about people who trusted God with their lives one day at a time. In the two books included in this seven-week study, Ruth and Esther, you will learn about people who trusted God not only for a day at a time, but for each moment as well. You will discover the results of their faith and the fulfillment of the plan God had for each of them from the time He formed them. "For Thou didst form my inward parts; Thou didst weave me in my mother's womb. I will give thanks to Thee, for I am fearfully and wonderfully made; wonderful are Thy works, and my soul knows it very well" (Ps. 139:13,14, *NASB*). He knows each one of us before we are even born. He has each one of us on His mind.

In the book of Ruth you will meet Naomi, Ruth and Boaz, people who trusted in the one true living God. As they faithfully walking in God's way, they in turn learned of His faithfulness. By the same token it is only through our everyday walk with the Lord that we discover God's faithfulness. Isaiah says it so well: "But those who hope in the Lord will renew their strength. They will soar on wings like eagles; they will run and not grow weary, they will walk and not faint" (40:31).

In part two of our study, you will meet Esther and Mordecai. The little orphan girl Esther and her cousin Mordecai, who adopted her as his own daughter after her parents died, are examples of people of faith, whose hope was in the Lord God. Surely their God, who had made the heavens and the earth, could renew their strength and show them how to courageously live in a pagan land where the one true God was not honored. Indeed they both had come to the kingdom of Persia "for such a time as this" (Esther 4:14).

Would you like to be "walking in God's way" every day of your life? May we encourage you to daily study the Bible along with the study questions and notes provided in this book. You will begin to rejoice as you see God's leading and providence in the lives of these men and women. At the same time you will see His hand in your life too!

"Ask where the good way is, and walk in it, and you will find rest for your souls" (Jer. 6:16).

HOW TO USE THIS BOOK

The Bible is a living book! It is relevant and powerful, but more than that, it is the active voice of our living God, and He wants to communicate with you daily through His Word. As you study the Bible, you will learn about God's person and character. You will begin to find His purpose for your life as He speaks to you through His written Word. His purpose is unchanging and His principles are unfailing guidelines for living. He will show us His truth and what our response should be to it.

Will you set aside a special time each day to interact with God in His Word? As you read, study, meditate and memorize His Word, the Holy Spirit will guide you, and His direction for your life will be made clear. More and more, His voice will be easily discerned in the din of life's pressures. When your heart is available and you see God's good intentions for you, you will then learn how to respond to the Lord's individual call to you day by day, moment by moment. As you train your ears to hear the voice of God, you will recognize His presence in the most unlikely circumstances and places. "The grass withers and the flowers fall, but the word of our God stands forever" (Isa. 40:8, *NIV*).

Will you choose to hear from God today? Open your Bible and turn to the study questions in Lesson 1. It is good to read the passage in several versions of the Bible, if you have them available. Each version may add new insights. Try not to use a commentary or any other reference book until you have allowed the Lord to personally speak to you from His word.

At the beginning of each set of questions, you will find suggestions for getting the most from your study of God's Word.

There are six sections of questions in each lesson. You will find it most beneficial to do one section daily. This will allow you time to meditate on God's Word and really hear what He has to say to you personally. When you have completed the questions, carefully read the study notes, which follow, and look up the Scripture verses. This

9

will give you added insight on the lesson you have just completed.

This study is designed to be used individually or in a group. If you're studying in a group, we urge you to actively share your answers and thoughts. In sharing we give encouragement to others and learn from one another.

May God bless you as you begin your journey into His Word. This may be the first time for you to take this trip, or it may be that you have journeyed this way many times before. No matter what trip it is for you, we pray you will find new joy and hope as you seek to live in the light of the living God!

PART 1

RUTH

1. A Tale of Love
2. Love's Rich Dividends

BY RUTH M. BATHAUER

1375 BC

RUTH, NAOMI   BOAZ

1050 BC

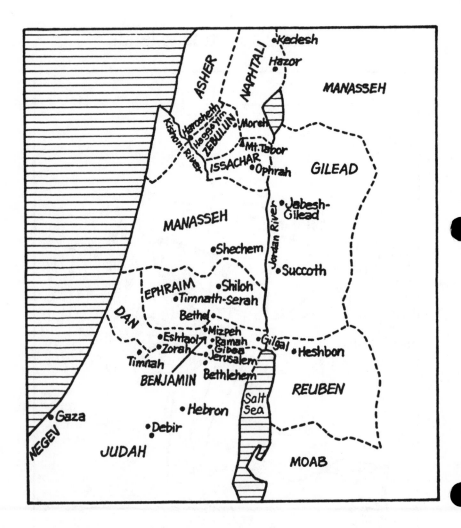

A TALE OF LOVE
RUTH 1 AND 2

Before you begin your study this week:
1. Pray and ask God to speak to you through His Holy Spirit each day.
2. Use only your Bible for your answers.
3. Write your answers and the verses you have used.
4. Challenge questions are for those who have the time and wish to do them.
5. Personal questions are to be shared with your study group only if you wish to share.
6. As you study look for a verse to memorize this week. Write it down, carry it with you, tack it to your bulletin board, tape it to the dashboard of your car. Make a real effort to learn the verse and its reference.

FIRST DAY: Read Ruth 1:1-11

1. Why did Elimelech and Naomi leave their hometown and move to Moab?

2. How long did the family live in Moab?

3. What was some of the sorrow Naomi experienced in Moab? Give the verses.

4. What made Naomi decide to go back to her hometown?

5 a. If you were in Naomi's sandals and had experienced what she had in these verses, what do you think might be some of your feelings?

b. As believers in Jesus Christ, what resources do we have in times of great sorrow that Naomi did not have? Read Hebrews 4:16; 12:2 and 13:5,6.

6. Why did Naomi urge her daughters-in-law to remain in their own homeland?

SECOND DAY: Read Ruth 2:1-13.

1. At this point, how did Naomi feel about herself? Note particularly Ruth 1:12,13,20,21 and jot down phrases that show how she felt.

2. What impressed you the most about Ruth's commitment found in Ruth 1:16,17? Why were you so impressed?

3. How were Ruth and Naomi received when they arrived in Bethlehem?

4. What clues do you find in these verses to show Naomi felt that God had been punishing her?

14

5 a. (Personal) Do you think Naomi's feelings were correct and that God did, in fact, punish her?

b. What encouragement do you find in John 16:33, as well as a fact about the Christian life on earth? Naomi did not have the Lord Jesus Christ's words to encourage her, but we have!

THIRD DAY: Read Ruth 2:1-13.

1. What specific information can you find in Ruth 2:1-4 that tells you something about Boaz? Give the answer in your own words and list the verses for your answer.

2. Where did Ruth go to find food, and what did she do?

3. What favorable report did the foreman give Boaz concerning Ruth's work?

4. What were some of the ways in which Boaz provided safety and security for Ruth?

5. Boaz recognized that Ruth was very poor, yet he was kind to her. What do the following verses say about God's care for the poor? Jot down a phrase (or use your own words) beside each reference.

Psalm 72:4

Psalm 102:17

Isaiah 14:30

Isaiah 41:17

6 a. **Challenge:** What do the following references say about the way we are to treat the poor? If you do not have time for all of these, find at least one Old Testament and one New Testament reference.

Psalm 41:1

Proverbs 28:27

Isaiah 1:17

Matthew 5:42

Mark 14:7

Ephesians 4:28

1 John 3:17

b. (Personal) How have these verses challenged you to help the poor in Christ's name? Please share with your group if possible.

FOURTH DAY: Read Ruth 2:14-23.

1. List several acts of kindness that Boaz showed to Ruth in this passage. Give the verses for your answer.

2. What does Naomi's comment tell you about her attitude now when she said, "The Lord has not stopped showing his kindness to the living and the dead"? (v. 20)

3. What promise does God give the Christian in Romans 8:28,29 that assures us that no matter how difficult our circumstances may be, God will not waste them?

4. (Personal) Could you share a personal experience of trial, illness or hardship where you, like Naomi, have seen that God has not left you, but is really there caring for you?

FIFTH DAY: Review Ruth 1,2.

1. In your opinion—as you skim Ruth 1—who do you feel acted as though she had the greater/stronger faith in God? Was it Ruth or Naomi? (see especially Ruth 1:16-18,20,21). Please give reasons for your answer.

2. Naomi was very concerned about her circumstances and felt that God was punishing her because He had deserted her. Can you find several verses in Ruth 2 indicating that God was, in fact, lovingly providing for both women? Do you think it was by chance that Ruth "happened" to go to Boaz's field?

3. (Personal) Have you ever felt the Lord has forgotten you? What message do you find that is especially for you in the following verses? How could these verses help you when you feel lonely or forgotten?

Joshua 1:9

Psalm 27:10

Psalm 48:14

Psalm 78:52

Isaiah 42:16

John 10:3,7

4. Please share your memory verse with your group. Also share why you chose this verse to add to your scriptural treasure chest.

SIXTH DAY: Read all the Notes and look up the Scriptures.

1. What new thought did you find helpful in the Notes?

2. What personal application did you select to apply to your own life this week?

Study Notes

How is your spiritual love life? On a scale of one to ten, how would you rate your concern for others? There is a price that comes with a sincere loving concern; unfortunately many followers of Christ are not ready to pay the price of self-sacrificing love for others.

Many of us need to ask the Lord daily to keep us from sliding to the low end of the scale where petty jealousy and envy take control—or where we're tempted to run when the going gets rough! Yet, the Bible frequently urges us to reach out in sincere loving concern. For example, "Little children, let us stop just *saying* we love people; let us *really* love them, and *show it* by our *actions*" (1 John 3:18, *TLB*).

You will find this thread of self-sacrificing love running throughout our study as we dig into the short but beautiful account found in the book of Ruth. We will see there was risk; there was a price that came with this unselfish love; but there was also a very great reward.

The account of Ruth is such a contrast to the preceding book of Judges. It is like a bright, sunny morning after a night of storm. Judges is filled with sin, war, strife and suffering. The book of Ruth centers around ordinary people and their love and concern for one another, as they face problems common to ordinary people.

Famine in the Land Ruth 1:1-5

The very first verse of the book of Ruth sets the scene for our study: "In the days when the judges ruled, there was a famine in the land." During the time of wars and strife described in the book of Judges, the events of Ruth's life were happening.

Ruth 1:1 gives no further explanation of what land, but for the Israelites there was only one land—the land God promised to His people—the Promised Land. With the promise of the land came the command that the Israelites were to stay close to the Lord their God and they were to listen to Him. "If . . . you will not listen to me, I will punish you for your sins . . . I will . . . make the sky above you like iron and the ground beneath you like bronze . . . your soil will not yield its crops, nor will the trees of the land yield their fruit" (Lev. 26:18-20). Apparently the famine mentioned in Ruth 1:1 was during one of the many times when the Israelites "again did evil in the sight of God" and He tried to get their attention by reminding them of His promises and their need for Him.

19

A Risky Move

While the book of Ruth is short, much information is packed into a few verses. In Ruth 1:1,2 we have our first introduction to the family; it is a family of four. We are told the names of all four and why they left their home in Bethlehem to go to Moab. Granted, living conditions in that day were often difficult under normal circumstances, but a famine would increase the hardship. Nothing in this passage, however, indicates that Elimelech and Naomi consulted God before leaving their home. Possibly the two decided on their own to do this.

The move was not without risk, for from the time of Moses, the descendants of Moab and Ammon were Israel's enemies. When Moses led the Israelites from Egypt, Moab and Ammon refused to give the Israelites bread and water. Later they hired a questionable prophet to curse the Israelites. As a result of their sins, God issued a strong edict against both Moab and Ammon (see Deut. 23:3-7). However, things apparently went fairly well for Naomi and her family in Moab for a time.

Tragedy Strikes

The phrase in the *New American Standard Bible*, "went to *sojourn* in the land of Moab" (Ruth 1:1) is important, for the word sojourn implies that they planned to return to Bethlehem—perhaps when the famine ended. Whether or not they planned to stay as long as they did (Ruth 1:4 says they stayed 10 years), while they were in Moab, tragedy struck.

First, Elimelech, the head of the household, died, leaving Naomi and her two sons. We don't know how old they were, but before long they married two girls, Orpah and Ruth, from Moab. Like any other mother, Naomi must have been happy about their marriages and was looking forward to grandchildren. Unfortunately, tragedy struck again—both of Naomi's sons died. So Naomi grieved not only for her husband, but also for her two sons.

A Difficult Farewell Ruth 1:6-18

For Naomi the land of Moab now spelled only sorrow. There was nothing left in Moab for her but three graves. No doubt during her sorrow Naomi's thoughts often turned back to Bethlehem. Then good news! She heard that the famine "back home" had ended. Without benefit of a twentieth-century news media, news traveled slowly in that day. By the time Naomi heard the news, there may have been several good harvests in Bethlehem.

20

More sorrow lay ahead for Naomi, however. Going back home meant leaving her daughters-in-law, whom she had grown to love deeply. Following customs of the East, Orpah and Ruth walked partway with Naomi as they made their way down the road to the border

They really loved one another and they were ready to show it by their actions.

of Moab. During this walk, the discussion recorded in Ruth 1:8-15 took place. Notice the self-sacrificing love displayed by the women, a good demonstration of 1 John 3:18—they really loved one another and they were ready to show it by their actions. Apparently both girls loved Naomi as deeply as she loved them, for they were ready to leave their homeland and go to Bethlehem with her. What a beautiful tribute to Naomi, the mother-in-law.

A Mother's Concern

Naomi was concerned for the future of her daughters-in-law and rightly so. The life of a widow in that day was very hard. Naomi's questions and comments in Ruth 1:11-12 have reference to a custom of that day that will be discussed more fully in a later lesson. Briefly, if one brother in a family died and his widow was left childless, another brother in the family was expected to marry his brother's widow. Much as Naomi loved both girls, she reminded them of her age and that there were no other sons in her family whom the girls could marry.

Orpah's action and personality suffer somewhat in contrast to Ruth, but she should not be criticized. She acted upon the advice of Naomi and returned to Moab. By doing so she dropped out of the biblical record. Not so with Ruth. Notice her commitment. She would not be persuaded to return. With complete self-sacrifice and devotion, she chose to go with her mother-in-law. She was well aware of the situation—she didn't stay for the sake of a future husband, but because of her sincere love for Naomi. Mothers-in-law have been the brunt of cruel jokes and put-downs for so long, thus this scene is especially refreshing. Apparently Ruth found in Naomi as much love and devotion as she had found in her own mother.

"Where You Go I Will Go"

Being older and wiser, Naomi knew what lay ahead in Israel for a young widow from Moab. She tried once more to encourage Ruth to go back with Orpah to their own people. Ruth's response in Ruth 1:16, 17 is perhaps the best known portion of the entire book of Ruth. We have all been touched by hearing these beautiful words of commitment recited at wedding ceremonies. Perhaps we have not realized what was involved for the young widow who so confidently spoke these words. Her love and devotion carried a great price.

Ruth's choice could mean that her own friends and relatives would cut her off. Due to racial problems between Moab and Israel, she could find herself unwanted in Israel. By choosing to go into enemy country, she would lose her rights as a citizen in her own nation. Are you beginning to understand the tremendous commitment Ruth made?

Would you be willing to give up your own people, your home, your citizenship, your homeland and follow a loved one into an enemy country? It would be like a U.S. citizen giving up all of his precious freedom to live in a communist land like Russia. Or a Russian defecting to the United States, knowing he could never return home, and taking the risk that his family back home would be tortured because he defected. What love! This is the love Ruth displayed for Naomi.

Not only did Ruth's choice have cultural overtones, but it involved religion as well. In Moab the people worshiped the Chemosh idol (see Num. 21:29). Ruth could not practice Chemosh worship in Israel. Perhaps Naomi and her sons had been such good witnesses of the Lord God that Ruth was drawn to Him more than the idols of Moab. Faithfully she made her choice, apparently knowing full well it meant she was cutting herself off from her own people in Moab and the idols they worshiped.

Ruth may still have been a "babe" or a new follower. Perhaps there were many things she didn't understand about the Lord, but Ruth wanted to follow Him! Centuries later Jesus Christ said, "Any of you who does not give up everything he has cannot be my disciple" (Luke 14:33). Ruth did "give up" all for Him. End of discussion! With Ruth's statements, Naomi realized there was no turning back for Ruth (see Ruth 1:18).

Home at Last! Ruth 1:19-22

No other details of their journey are given, but Ruth and Naomi created quite a stir when they reached Bethlehem. Since they arrived at the beginning of the barley harvest (see Ruth 1:22), it is possible the men were out in the fields. If it were toward evening, the women of Bethlehem, following the custom of the day, were probably gathered at the city well where business, news and gossip were usually exchanged.

Remember, at least 10 years had gone by since her friends had seen Naomi. The years had not been easy—Naomi suffered great sorrow. Perhaps her hair had turned gray and the lines of sorrow were heavy upon her face. No doubt the conversation among the Bethlehem women buzzed when Ruth and Naomi arrived. With a bit of speculation, we can imagine the comments: "She really has aged!" or "Poor Naomi must have suffered!" While Scripture does not tell us these actual comments, if you look at Ruth 1:19 you get a good description of their homecoming: "The whole town was stirred," and "Can this be Naomi?"

To understand Ruth 1:20 we need to know that great emphasis was placed upon names in that day. Names were thought to describe the individual—the name Naomi means "pleasant" while Mara means "bitter." Verses 20 and 21 lead us to believe, as mentioned earlier, that Naomi and her husband may have left Bethlehem 10 years earlier without consulting the Lord. Perhaps this is why Naomi implies her loss is something of a punishment from God. She doesn't realize that, although her future looks dark, God is in fact at work in her life, even while she is judging herself and blaming God. At this point Naomi doesn't know that God has some of His very richest blessings in store for her. Instead of confessing her feelings to the Lord, Naomi tells her friends, "The Lord has afflicted me; the Almighty has brought misfortune upon me" (Ruth 1:21).

Whether or not the death of Naomi's husband and sons was a punishment (I personally do not believe it was), we do know that God the Father suffers with us when we suffer. He is a God of compassion. Isaiah says, "In all their [God's people's] distress he too was distressed . . . In his love and mercy . . . he lifted them up and carried them all the days of old" (63:9).

God Will Never Leave You

In my friend's home is a beautiful picture depicting footprints on a sandy beach with ocean waves gently rolling onto the sand. I discovered this picture was inspired by the following story written by an unknown author: I dreamed I was walking along the beach with the Lord. Scenes from my life flashed before me. In each scene I noticed two sets of footprints in the sand—one belonging to me, the other to the Lord. Then I noticed that many times there was only one set of footprints. This was distressing to me, for I noticed that the one set of footprints occurred at the very lowest and saddest times in my life. Disappointed and hurt, I prayed to Him, "Lord, you promised that if I followed you, you would walk with me always. But I see during the most troublesome times in my life, there is only one set of footprints.

I don't understand why in times when I needed you most you would leave." To which the Lord replied, "My precious child, I will never leave you! When you see only one set of footprints, it was then that I *carried* you!"

In the book of Habakkuk, the prophet cries out to the Lord complaining of the situation in which he finds himself. "How long, O Lord, must I call for help, but you do not listen?" (1:2; read the rest of Habakkuk's complaints in verses 1-4). Then comes the Lord's gracious, loving reply. "Look . . . and be utterly amazed. For I am going to do something in your days *that you would not believe, even if you were told*" (1:5, italics added).

The same was true for Naomi. Even while she was complaining, God was at work. God had so many rich blessings in store for her that Naomi would not have believed even if God had revealed them to her at that moment! Unfortunately most of us are guilty of doing the same thing Naomi did. We become discouraged and ready to give up, declaring life to be "bitter and empty" and all the time God is at work, eager to guide us into blessings if we would only trust Him and allow Him to do so. God is almighty and sovereign; He is able to make all things work together for good for His children (see Rom. 8:28).

The Lord Orders Our Steps Ruth 2:1-7

The Bible offers no details on the grief Ruth must have been suffering during that time—she too lost her husband. She was in a foreign land. She had no idea how she, a Moabite widow, would be accepted in the land of Israel. In these verses we see another side of Ruth's fine character. There was no social security or welfare in those days. Ruth must have known it was up to her to earn the food she and Naomi needed. Instead of wallowing in self-pity at her losses, Ruth took the initiative and asked Naomi, "Let me go to the fields and pick up the leftover grain behind anyone in whose eyes I find favor" (Ruth 2:2).

Harvest was usually a seven-week period, lasting from mid-April to mid-June. It meant a great deal of hard work and long hours. Men went through the fields grabbing hands full of grain and cutting the stalks with sickles. Small bunches of grain were tied into bundles called sheaves. As the men worked a number of grain stalks fell to the ground. These stray stalks could also be gathered, but according to the law of Moses, poor people were permitted to follow the harvesters and gather the stalks that were dropped. In fact landowners were instructed, "You shall not reap to the very corners of your field, neither shall you gather the gleanings of your harvest" (Lev. 19:9, *NASB*).

The same was true when harvesting fruit—some was to be left

for the poor (see Lev. 19:10; 23:22 and Deut. 24:19). Often these gleanings were all that stood between poor people and starvation. And they earned their food; it was backbreaking work to stoop again and again to gather the grain while the hot sun streamed down upon the workers.

Ruth went out in faith—expecting, anticipating to find something. She didn't wait for the Lord to drop the work into her lap.

While Ruth may not have been aware of His leading, we know the Bible says, "The steps of a good man [or woman] are ordered by the Lord" (Ps. 37:23, *KJV*). Thus we read, "As it turned out, she found herself working in the field belonging to Boaz" (Ruth 2:3). Her father-in-law, Elimelech, had come from a wealthy family and Boaz was one of the rich relatives who lived in Bethlehem. Was it by chance that Ruth found herself in the field of Naomi's rich relative? Not by any means! Ruth was led to that field as surely as Eliezer, the servant of Abraham, was led to find a bride for Isaac. Eliezer said, "I being in the way, the Lord led me" (Gen. 24:27, *KJV*).

God Promises to Guide Believers

The Lord's guidance is promised to every believer. Notice, however, that Ruth went out in faith—expecting, anticipating to find something. She didn't wait for the Lord to drop the work into her lap. She had made a commitment to Naomi and to God when she left Moab and she continued to follow through. Think for a moment. Can you recall some experience in your own life when you were not particularly aware of God's leading and yet some small incident occurred that changed your entire life? If you are walking with the Lord, if you are in the Word and ask for His guidance, He will direct you just as He led Ruth to that specific field. As we acknowledge our need for Him, He will direct our paths—for He has promised He would (see Prov. 3:5-6).

A missionary tells of an experience he had while visiting numerous tribal mission stations in Zaire, Africa. During his travels he came near the home he and his family had built near a lake. He went there to spend the night. Because the house had been empty for some time, looters had invaded it and many of the missionary's belongings had been stolen.

Early the next morning, as he filled a can with fresh lake water, the missionary noticed a native fisherman on shore. The scene reminded the missionary of an outboard motor he'd left in his storeroom. Wondering whether it too had been stolen, he went to investigate. As he entered the storeroom, he suddenly felt a red-hot liquid sprayed into his eye—the work of a spitting cobra, one of the most deadly, poisonous snakes in the world!

The missionary ran screaming outside, stumbling over the five-gallon can of fresh water he'd gotten earlier. Frantically he splashed water into his eyes. His screams brought the native fisherman who, when he saw what had happened, ran for help. Two white people responded. One woman was a nurse who carried a sample of eye medicine she'd received in the mail a few days earlier. The nurse administered the medication while the white man killed the cobra. Suddenly a French doctor on his way to a diamond mine happened on the scene. He'd stopped to see the beautiful Lake Munkamba, where the missionary's home was located. When the doctor heard what happened he told them of a new antibiotic that had just been released; unfortunately, he had no medication with him. When the nurse produced the sample medication, the French doctor shouted, "That's it! That's the one I was telling you about!"

After much rest and using the sample medication, the missionary's life was spared and his eyesight restored. Notice how many events happened at just the right moment—the fresh water, the native African, the missionary nurse and her guest, the doctor, the sample medication. A coincidence? No. The moving of a great God who cares for His own!

A Kind and Just Boss Ruth 2:8-17

Ruth 2:4 introduces us to the landowner, Boaz, who came into the field where Ruth was working. From the way he greeted his laborers, we immediately learn that Boaz was a man of God: "The Lord be with you!" From their response, we are led to believe there was a good relationship between Boaz and his workers. Apparently Boaz knew each of his workers by name and perhaps even by family.

As he scanned his laborers, he noticed the attractive stranger. His foreman told Boaz, "She is the Moabitess" (Ruth 2:6). There is just a hint of slander in the reply—"She's that foreigner who came back with Naomi from Moab!" By carefully reading, we note that any attempt at slander was thoroughly squelched by Boaz. While the foreman was quick to admit to the diligence of Ruth's work, Boaz must have been quick to give clear instructions to his men (see Ruth 2:8,16).

No doubt Boaz had heard of Ruth and her kindness to Naomi, but this was perhaps the first time he had met her. He liked what he saw and invited her to remain in his field for the rest of the season. Read Ruth 2:8,9 to see what further security Boaz provided. There was to be no question among his workers how Boaz felt about Ruth. It is likely his protection was partially due to his appreciation for what Ruth had done for Naomi.

Already Ruth's commitment of doing good in the name of the Lord was paying dividends. Jesus said, "Whatever you did for one of the least of these brothers of mine, you did for me" (Matt. 25:40). Ruth gave up all she had to follow Naomi and the God of Israel, and one can never out give the Lord. When a good deed is done in His name, He will repay. At this moment Ruth was beginning to experience His goodness. But this was only the beginning—there was much more to come!

Unselfish Commitment

Obviously, Ruth's commitment to Naomi was not for selfish reasons (see Ruth 2:10). The Hebrew word for "favor" in verse 10 means grace or kindness. From her question it is evident that Ruth felt she did not deserve this kindness and knew this was not the routine way foreigners were treated. Ruth's kind and loving concern for Naomi and her deep commitment to the Lord had already earned her the respect from Boaz. Notice the short benediction Boaz pronounced upon Ruth (Ruth 2:12). In his book *Judges and Ruth,* the biblical scholar Leon Morris says of the prayer, the "image is probably that of a tiny bird snuggling under the wings of a foster mother."

Ruth 2:12 is a word picture of trust and security. Perhaps Ruth reminded Boaz of a frightened little bird as she worked diligently searching for the food she and Naomi needed. Ruth may have expected the worst since she faced racial problems, was a widow, a stranger and foreigner in a new land; so the friendly words from Boaz were a great comfort (see Ruth 2:13).

Usually gleaners were only to work the edge and corners of the fields. Boaz, however, instructed his men to leave some of the grain especially for Ruth. We can see, from all these acts of kindness, that God was not only at work preparing the way for Ruth, God was also preparing the heart of Boaz and his role in Ruth's life, according to His sovereign will and purpose.

By the end of the day, through her hard work and Boaz's kindness, Ruth harvested "about an ephah" (Ruth 2:17)—approximately three pecks. There was enough food for Ruth and Naomi for almost a week—just from one day's work!

A Home Full of Joy and Praise Ruth 2:18-23

Naomi was well aware of the problems facing a foreigner who was out looking for work. No doubt she waited eagerly all day for Ruth's return that evening. Can you imagine Naomi's surprise at the large amount of grain plus part of Ruth's leftover lunch? After firing two questions in rapid succession at Ruth (see Ruth 2:19) Naomi shows her concern for her daughter-in-law. Before Ruth could answer the questions, or before she knew who Ruth's benefactor was, Naomi said, "Blessed be the man who took notice of you!" Someone had been kind to Ruth, the foreigner. Someone had given her an opportunity to work and find food!

Little by little Ruth relates her experiences and the kindness of Boaz. As Naomi hears the name of Boaz, a change comes over her attitude. No longer is she bitter and discouraged. Instead she begins to praise the Lord, "The Lord bless him!" God hadn't forgotten them! Naomi then explains the reason for her great pleasure. Boaz is a relative—"one of our kinsman-redeemers" (Ruth 2:20). This phrase refers back to an interesting law of redemption we will discuss and define in the next lesson. An excellent conclusion to Ruth 1 and 2 is to see a discouraged, bitter Naomi once more rejoice in the Lord as she says, "The Lord bless him! . . . The Lord has not stopped showing his kindness to the living and the dead" (v. 20).

LOVE'S RICH DIVIDENDS

RUTH 3 AND 4

Before you begin your study this week:
1. Pray and ask God to speak to you through His Holy Spirit each day.
2. Use only your Bible for your answers.
3. Write your answers and the verses you have used.
4. Challenge questions are for those who have the time and wish to do them.
5. Personal questions are to be shared with your study group only if you wish to share.
6. As you study look for a verse to memorize this week. Write it down, carry it with you, tack it to your bulletin board, tape it to the dashboard of your car. Make a real effort to learn the verse and its reference.

FIRST AND SECOND DAYS: Read Ruth 3

1. What was Naomi's deep concern for Ruth in Ruth 3:1?

2. Make a list of the things Naomi asked Ruth to do (see Ruth 3:3,4).

3. The role of women in Ruth's day was very different from the role of women today. What happened to change women's role? Base your answer on Galatians 3:26-28.

4. (Personal) What in Galatians 3:26-28 is most meaningful to you? Why?

5. What clue do you find in Ruth 3:10-13 that indicates Boaz was older than Ruth?

6. What compliment did Boaz pay Ruth concerning her godly testimony within Bethlehem?

7 a. (Personal) What are some of the clues that tell you a person you have just met might be a Christian?

   b. We can never fully know a person's relationship to God. There is One who knows. What does 1 Samuel 16:7 say to indicate that God always knows a person's heart attitude toward Christ even though we don't always know it?

   c. What does 2 Corinthians 3:3 say about our lives and our witness?

8. **Challenge:** Describe in your own words what Deuteronomy 25:5-10 says about a kinsman-redeemer.

9. What was Boaz's response to Ruth concerning his role as her kinsman-redeemer?

THIRD AND FOURTH DAYS: Read Ruth 4.

1. What business did Boaz have to take care of at the city gate, the place of official business?

2. What clue do you find in these verses that indicate Boaz was eager to take on the responsibility of Ruth's kinsman-redeemer?

3. What reason did the unnamed relative give for not becoming Ruth's kinsman-redeemer?

4. Which one of Naomi's sons had been Ruth's husband?

5. What was the meaning of the words of the well-wishers when they said to Boaz, "May the Lord make the woman who is coming into your home like Rachel and Leah"? (see Gen. 35:22-26).

6. What great blessing did Ruth and Naomi receive from God through their son Obed? Who was Obed's son? Who was Jesse's son? (see Ruth 4 and Matt. 1:5-6).

7. Boaz, the kinsman-redeemer, is a picture of what God has done for us through the Lord Jesus Christ, our Redeemer.

   a. What does John 3:16 tell you about God's love and what He did about His love for us?

b. What did Jesus Christ, our Redeemer, do for each one of us according to 1 Peter 2:24 and Colossians 1:20?

c. How is our position changed when we accept Christ as our own Redeemer? (see John 1:12 and 2 Cor. 5:17).

FIFTH DAY: Read Psalm 139:1-12; 17,18; 23,24.

One of the important messages found in the book of Ruth is that God was with Ruth and Naomi at all times, even when, for example, Naomi felt bitter and neglected and complained that God had punished her. God is always with you according to Psalm 139, whether you are always aware of His presence or not—He is there loving you!

1. What are some of the things the Lord already knows about you? (see especially Ps. 139:2-4).

2. What answer does the psalmist discover to his own question about getting away from God and His Spirit? List phrases from Psalm 139:8-12 that answer the psalmist's question.

3. **Challenge:** Psalm 139 gives us a beautiful picture of God. Read the psalm again and then decide which verses tell you that:

a. God is present everywhere

b. God is all-knowing

4. (Personal) What does the prayer in Psalm 139:23,24 mean to you? Is it a prayer you would like to make your own? Tell the Lord how you feel.

5. If you are studying with a group, share your memory verse with your discussion group. Also share the method you used to memorize this verse.

SIXTH DAY: Read all the Notes and look up the Scriptures.

1. What new thought did you find helpful in the Notes?

2. What personal application did you select to apply to your own life this week?

Study Notes

Have you ever had to leave friends and loved ones and move to another state or to another city? If you have, can you recall your feelings of apprehension and loneliness at facing a new job, finding Christian friends or enrolling in a new school?

I was 10 years old when my family moved, and I had to change schools. How I dreaded it! I was a very shy child and it wasn't easy for me to make friends. My mother reminded me frequently that the Lord would be with me. We talked often about making new friends and how the Lord would prepare the way. How well I remember the evening prior to the first day at my new school. While Mom and I prepared dinner, we again talked about the next day, and then together we sang that old gospel hymn that says, in effect, "If Jesus goes with me, I can go anywhere!"

Some of these same feelings must have been in the heart of the unknown poet who wrote these lines:

> God is your Father, Redeemer and Friend,
> He is the faithful One, true to the end;
> Guiding, protecting, and keeping His own,
> He cannot fail you—so trust Him alone.
>
> Anonymous

This is an excellent description of the Lord's hand upon the lives of Ruth and Naomi. Whether or not they were always aware of Him, He did guide and protect them as His own. Perhaps Ruth had feelings of apprehension and loneliness as she left her home in Moab and became exposed more fully to the teachings of the God of Israel and to some of the unfamiliar customs and traditions of Naomi's people, which we will discover in our study of Ruth chapters 3 and 4.

Two Women on Their Own Ruth 3:1

The two months of barley harvest were quickly coming to an end and Naomi was deeply concerned for her daughter-in-law and for their welfare. Where would they find food after the harvest? Jobs were not readily available.

In that day the role of the woman was far different from what it is today, and both Ruth and Naomi were far from being the "liberated women" of our century. Then a woman was first and foremost a wife and mother. While a wife called her husband "lord" or "master" (see Gen. 18:12; Judg. 19:26), she was still on a far higher level than a slave. A man could sell his slave—but never his wife!

34

A woman earned her husband's respect by doing the hard work at home: tending the flocks, working in the fields, spinning, cooking, etc. (see Prov. 31:10-31). Giving birth to children, especially sons, increased her respect in the eyes of her husband, and children were expected to show as much respect to their mother as to their father (see Exod. 20:12; 21:17; Lev. 20:9, Deut. 21:18-21). Because of the woman's role as a wife and mother, a widow had a very difficult time on her own.

Women Are Free in Christ

Why has the role of women changed so greatly in our day? Is it due to our twentieth-century women's liberation movement? No! A thousand times no! As women we have been truly liberated because the *Lord Jesus Christ* has set us free! He accomplished this liberation through His victorious death on the cross and in His resurrection.

By faith in Him we may become children of God. The Bible says, "You are all sons [children] of God through faith in Christ Jesus" and it says we have been clothed with Christ. "There is neither Jew nor Greek, slave nor free, *male nor female,* for you are *all one* in Christ Jesus" (see Gal. 3:26-28, italics added). Because we are on this side of the cross, God sees no sexual distinction among His children.

> ### The husband is to love his wife as Christ loved the Church.

It was Christ who raised the role of the woman to a place never known in the ancient world. While the Bible pattern is for the man to be the head of the home—the leader—and the woman to be submissive to him (see Eph. 5:21-33), at the same time the husband is to love his wife as Christ loved the Church. And Galatians 3:26-29 tells us that women are spiritually equal with men in God's sight.

Women and men are on an equal level when it comes to receiving spiritual blessings. Moslem women, however, still do not have this equal status under their religion—nor do women in many other religions. Why not take a moment right now to earnestly thank the Lord Jesus for what He has done for women.

As we come to Ruth chapter 3 it is interesting to compare verse 1 as given in three of the prominent Bible versions: *King James* says, "Shall I not seek rest for thee, that it may be well with thee?" The *New American Standard Bible* says, "Shall I not seek security for you?" while the *New International Version* says, "Should I not try to find a home for you, where you will be well provided for?" All are correct translations, but it seems the *NIV* is especially good in view of what a concerned mother would say in loving concern for her daughter-in-law.

Since Naomi herself was also a widow, you might question why she was not concerned with finding a husband for herself. Naomi, however, already answered that question when she said, "I am too old to have another husband" (Ruth 1:12). Naomi is ready to take second place and, in love, help Ruth find a future and a home.

May Your Love Increase

All of us might make 1 Thessalonians 3:12 our prayer: "May the Lord make your love increase and overflow for each other and for everyone else." If this love were typical in our present-day homes and family relationships, what a different world we would have. It is not easy to deny ourselves and to let our love grow. We can only do it through the power of the Holy Spirit living within us.

When Frederick Arnot, missionary explorer, was traveling with a group of his African converts, one of the young men was suddenly attacked by a lion. Immediately Arnot went into action. He pushed the young man to the ground and threw himself over the youth. No doubt Arnot uttered a prayer to his heavenly Father even as he tried physically to protect the African. For some unknown reason—except for God's intervention—the lion backed off and did not attempt to attack Arnot. Needless to say, Arnot became a hero among the African tribe. "I'd go anywhere with a white man who would put his own body between a lion and his black friend," said the chief when he heard the report of the brave rescue.

Plan Your Work . . .

All during harvest while Ruth was busy gleaning in Boaz's fields, perhaps Naomi had been making plans of her own concerning Ruth's future. Long before she shared the plans with Ruth, Naomi may have discussed these plans with the Lord, for the ideas listed in Ruth chapter 3 indicate very careful, thorough planning. What better home or "rest" for Ruth than Boaz, who had already shown a great deal of interest in her with special favors as she worked in his fields. Naomi shares, step-by-step, what was to be done, for she was well-acquainted with the Israelite method of harvest and their wedding customs.

To "winnow" the barley (see Ruth 3:2) the sheaves were scattered over a threshing floor—a hard, dry, flat piece of ground. To

36

loosen the kernels and break the stalks into chaff, oxen were driven over the stalks, or the stalks were beaten by hand, or animals were hitched to a wooden sled and the sled was pulled over the stalks. Finally, the winnowers tossed the mixture into the air against the wind so that the lighter chaff was blown away and the heavier grain fell to the ground.

Naomi knew that Boaz would be out on the threshing floor at night. During harvesttime the Midianites and Amalekites often invaded the land, robbing the people of the threshed grain, so to protect their harvest, the Israelites slept on the threshing floor during the winnowing. While the work was hard, winnowing was also a festive time, a time of celebration and thanksgiving for the Lord's provision. The timing was perfect for Naomi's plans; if the grain was plentiful, Boaz would be in a receptive mood.

. . . Work Your Plan

Note Naomi's careful instructions to Ruth in Ruth 3:3,4. The two widows might have been poor, but Ruth was to put on her "best clothes" for the occasion. Some biblical scholars believe that "best clothes" may refer to a large mantle Ruth was to wear to hide her identity until the right moment. At any rate, Ruth was not to approach Boaz until he had eaten and retired. Naomi had thought of everything, for many women know the futility of approaching a hungry man for a decision!

To our twentieth-century minds it is difficult to understand what Naomi was asking Ruth to do. She is not suggesting anything improper or immoral. Ruth was to wait until Boaz had retired, then she was to slip over to him and lie at his feet—a position of humility. When Boaz discovered her, Ruth was to follow his instructions.

Have you ever been asked to do something unfamiliar to you and you weren't quite sure how it would be received? Perhaps Ruth also had questions, for remember, she is now living among people whose customs may appear strange to her. Questions or not, Ruth agrees to obey. She was being true to her commitment she'd made back in Moab.

It Pays to Follow Through Ruth 3:5-10

Following Naomi's instructions, Ruth took a position where she could watch Boaz as he finished his meal and settled down for the night. After a hard day's work he was soon sound asleep. That was Ruth's signal and she went quietly to lie down at his feet.

During the night something startled Boaz and he discovered a woman lying at his feet! Imagine his surprise. No doubt he went to

37

sleep with thoughts of robbers and enemies, and protecting his grain. Now abruptly awakened he demanded, "Who are you?" (Ruth 3:9).

Ruth immediately told him her name, but she takes nothing for granted. She maintained her spirit of humility as she called herself "your servant." Then in the same breath she said, "Spread the corner of your garment over me, since you are a kinsman-redeemer" (v.9).

In order to understand what Ruth meant, we need to know that it was an ancient custom for a bridegroom to cover his bride with his *talith*, a fringed garment, as a symbol of his protection and authority (see Ezek. 16:8). The word *kinsman-redeemer* is an interesting term that refers back to a law of redemption of a childless widow (see Deut. 25:5-10). Under this law, the kinsman was to marry the widow and raise a son to keep alive the name of the dead husband.

A man's name was very important, so a kinsman-redeemer was a legal arrangement. The kinsman was usually a brother, or the very next of kin, and he really had little choice in the matter—except to refuse and take the consequences as described in Deuteronomy.

It is the Spirit of God shining through our lives that causes our friends and neighbors to know we belong to Him.

In light of this custom, Boaz saw nothing strange or unbecoming in Ruth's actions. Instead, he praises her conduct. Ruth had proven herself a godly woman by taking care of Naomi and by her modest conduct as she worked in the fields. And her actions that night were in accordance with the Levitical marriage laws. He commends Ruth for choosing to keep her family relationship through the nearest relative and for her loyalty to Naomi, rather than running after "younger men, whether rich or poor" (Ruth 3:10).

A Promise of Marriage Ruth 3:11-18

A careful reading of the rest of the chapter gives us an insight into the personality of Boaz. He must have been a sensitive, kind, observant person. While considerably older than Ruth, he obviously had noticed her modest behavior during the weeks she had been working in his fields. Apparently God had already planted a deep love for Ruth in Boaz's heart. His words, "Don't be afraid" imply his understanding of Ruth's coming to him. No doubt he heard fear in her voice as she followed Naomi's instruction in this Israelite custom. It took courage to do what she was told to do, even though it was unfamiliar to her.

Without hesitation Boaz agrees to give Ruth complete protection.

He further gives her a compliment for her beautiful godly witness when he says, "All my fellow townsmen know that you are a woman of noble character" (Ruth 3:11). As a foreigner and a widow, she could easily have been molested while working in the fields, but her actions portrayed to all she belonged to the living God.

What Do Our Actions Reveal?

What about our own actions, words and attitudes? Whether you are a new Christian or a Christian of many years, what is your community saying about you? Is it evident you belong to the living God? The apostle Paul says, "You show that you are a letter from Christle . . . written not with ink but with the Spirit of the living God" (2 Cor. 3:3). It is the Spirit of God shining through our lives that causes our friends and neighbors to know we belong to Him.

Nothing Worthwhile Comes Easy

Apparently Boaz had been thinking of Ruth as more than just one of the servant girls working in his fields, for he immediately points out a problem. There was a man who was a closer relative than Boaz. Had Ruth's action been a complete surprise, would Boaz have been so quick to think of the closer relative? Some biblical scholars believe Boaz was a nephew of Elimelech. Jewish law carefully stipulated that the kinsman-redeemer was to be a blood relative. If for some reason—such as sickness, a mental problem, or insufficient funds—the nearest blood relative could not assume this responsibility, then the next man in line could become the kinsman-redeemer.

It was no easy thing to take on the role of kinsman-redeemer. The man filling that role may already have a family of his own; but if his brother died, the kinsman-redeemer had to continue caring for his own family, as well as take over all of his brother's possessions: land, houses, business, and any mortgages and debts. As we've already mentioned, a kinsman was also required to father a son so that his brother's name would be kept alive. A portion of the inheritance would go to this son and not to the kinsman-redeemer.

Eager as Boaz was to redeem Ruth and provide protection for her, he had to work within the law of that day (see Ruth 3:12). So he insisted that the closer relative be given first choice. The unspoken message of Boaz's love for Ruth is nevertheless clear as he assures her that if the nearest relative chooses not to redeem her, "I vow that, as surely as the Lord lives, I will do it" (Ruth 3:13).

Notice, too, the time factor. Boaz was not willing to expose Ruth to a time of waiting. He wanted to settle the matter as quickly as possible—in fact, he would take care of it the very next morning.

It's So Hard to Wait

Still the perfect gentleman, Boaz wanted to protect Ruth's good name and reputation, thus he suggested she leave for home before dawn, under cover of darkness, so she would not be recognized. Although there was nothing immoral about her visit, Boaz was concerned lest people misunderstand. Before sending her home, Boaz gave Ruth "six measures of barley"—another indication of his feelings for her.

One of the remarkable facts about Ruth was her openness with Naomi. Showing her gift of barley, Ruth "told her everything Boaz had done for her" (Ruth 3:16). Naomi apparently knew Boaz quite well and she told Ruth to wait, "For the man will not rest until the matter is settled today" (Ruth 3:18).

"Wait" is perhaps one of the most difficult things to do when the heart and emotions are involved. Yet how important for us to wait for the Lord to guide in matters of marriage and love. How many broken homes and hearts could be avoided if more young people—older ones too!—would wait for the Lord's leading before rushing into marriage.

Waiting—But Don't Sit Idly By Ruth 4:1-8

True to his word, Boaz immediately set the wheels in motion for settling the problem of redemption. Ruth 4:1 says he went to the city gate. In that day the city gate was like our city hall. It was the place where government and business transactions were conducted. One of the most important functions of the gate was its judicial activity: there, laws were made and people were sentenced before the elders—even execution sentences were issued there (see Deut. 22:15,24).

Boaz took "ten of the elders of the town" (Ruth 4:2). These men would serve as jury, and were required for the marriage benediction. In the presence of these 10 men and the general public, the proceedings started when the nearest relative, whose name is never given, arrived. No doubt there was tension. If a kinsman refused to take on his responsibility, the rejected widow could, according to law, take off one of the kinsman's sandals in public, spit in his face and say, "This is what is done to the man who will not build up his brother's family line!" (Deut. 25:9).

While he was willing to abide by law and give the nearest kinsman his rightful first choice, Boaz himself was very eager to assume the responsibility for the lovely Ruth. By announcing that the land belonging to Elimelech was for sale, Boaz gave his opponent a chance to buy

40

it. The phrase "our brother Elimelech" in Ruth 4:3 should be translated, "friend." Boaz is quick to add that if the relative is not interested in buying, "Tell me, so I will know . . . . For . . . I am next in line" (Ruth 4:4). The unnamed kinsman apparently assumed that the land belonged only to Naomi and that his responsibility would end with the purchase of it, so he agreed to buy.

Disappointments Along the Way

Perhaps at that very moment Boaz saw his dreams of a wonderful future with Ruth crumble before him! Read Ruth 4:5 and notice how quickly Boaz spells out further stipulations concerning the obligation of redemption. It meant more responsibility for the kinsman—not only was Naomi involved, but he would "acquire" Ruth, a Moabitess, a stranger from a despised people. Since Ruth had no son, the possibility of fathering a son who would not be pure Jewish but would have Moabite blood in his veins was unthinkable! Further, the kinsman would face a financial loss, for he would have to spend money for land that would not belong to him, but eventually would belong to Ruth's son.

As his responsibilities are spelled out, the kinsman's enthusiasm suddenly evaporated. The price was too great. As quickly as he decided to buy the land, the kinsman did a complete about-face. He didn't want to "endanger" his own estate. He almost begged Boaz to assume the role of kinsman-redeemer. Taking off his sandal was an old symbolic custom of transfer. The man who took off his sandal renounced any legal rights he had in a matter. The ball was finally in Boaz's court. At last he was free to legally take on the role of kinsman-redeemer not only for Naomi, but also for his beloved Ruth.

Determination Pays Off Ruth 4:9-21

No doubt there were three very happy people in Bethlehem that day—Boaz, Ruth and Naomi. Ruth 4:9,10 gives Boaz's public declaration that he has taken over the property and has assumed sole responsibility for both Ruth and Naomi. For the first time we discover which of Naomi's sons Ruth had married (Ruth 4:10). Continuing to follow the law, Boaz announces the purpose and result of the transaction, "In order to maintain the name of the dead with his property, so that his name will not disappear."

Well wishes from friends and witnesses rang out for the happy couple. "Rachel and Leah" were the wives of Jacob, and the witnesses expressed the prayer that Boaz would be rewarded with a family as large as that of Jacob—who had 12 sons (Gen. 35:22-26).

41

Ruth's choice to follow the living God rewarded her with many rich blessings. Her name was changed, her position was changed—now she belonged to her kinsman-redeemer who could provide for her needs. God blessed this marriage and gave them a son. Through this son, Ruth finally became the great grandmother of David.

God's Message of Love to You

The entire book of Ruth is a beautiful picture of what God has done for you—for us! First of all we see the greatness and sovereignty of God. As God led Naomi, Ruth and Boaz and brought their lives together, He established a family through whom He would send the Savior into our sinful world. (Note carefully the lineage of Jesus in Matt. 1.) Ruth's great desire was to follow God and to please Him (see Ruth 1:16,17). As Ruth's life unfolds in the book, see how it depicts the born-again believer who through faith in Christ has found new life! Who can deny God's leading all the way in both Ruth and Naomi's lives?

A Picture of Christ

Boaz, the kinsman-redeemer, is a picture of our Lord and Savior, Jesus Christ. Boaz loved Ruth, a foreigner, just as she was, and he was willing to reach down to her in her poverty. He saw her problem and her need and was eager to become her kinsman-redeemer. Lifting her out of her poverty, Boaz made her his own to love and care for.

Do you realize what God has done for you? Because of His great love (see John 3:16), He sent His Son Jesus to earth as a baby (see Luke 2). He became man and took upon Himself our sins (see 1 Pet. 2:24) and paid the full price so that He might bring us to God (see Col. 1:20). Through His death our position has been changed, for we are sons of God (see John 1:12) and new persons in Christ (see 2 Cor. 5:17).

Read again Ruth's commitment in Ruth 1:16,17. Is the living God your God? Have you chosen to follow Him? Are "your people" born-again believers? What is the Lord Jesus to you? All of this new life is available to you, but you must choose to have it. You must admit you have a need for a Redeemer who can break the power of sin over you, who can bring you to God and make you His own. What is your choice?

PART 2

ESTHER

3. A Queen Is Dethroned
4. A New Queen Is Chosen
5. For Such a Time as This
6. Our Perfect Strength and Shield
7. A Marvelous Deliverance

BY DORIS W. GREIG

460 BC

VASHTI   ESTHER   HAMAN / MORDECAI

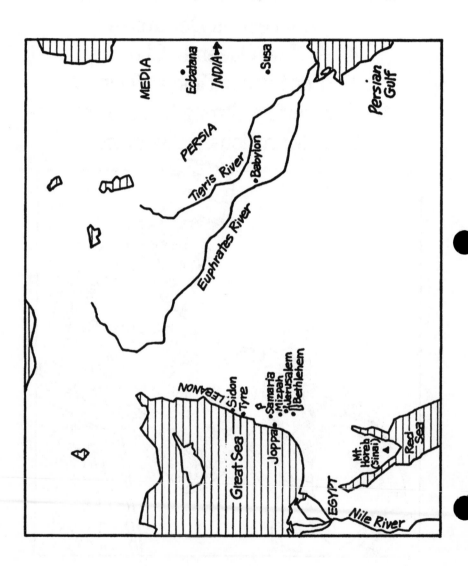

MEDIA

Ecbatana

INDIA →

Susa

PERSIA

Persian Gulf

Tigris River

Babylon

Euphrates River

LEBANON

Sidon

Tyre

Samaria

Mizpah

Jerusalem

Bethlehem

Great Sea

Joppa

Mt. Horeb (Sinai)

Red Sea

EGYPT

Nile River

A QUEEN IS DETHRONED

ESTHER 1

Before you begin your study this week:
1. Pray and ask God to speak to you through His Holy Spirit each day.
2. Use only your Bible for your answers.
3. Write your answers and the verses you have used.
4. Challenge questions are for those who have the time and wish to do them.
5. Personal questions are to be shared with your study group only if you wish to share.
6. As you study look for a verse to memorize this week. Write it down, carry it with you, tack it to your bulletin board, tape it to the dashboard of your car. Make a real effort to learn the verse and its reference.

FIRST DAY: Read Esther 1 concentrating on verses 1-8.

1 a. Over what areas did Ahasuerus reign and where was his capital in Persia?

b. What did this king do in the third year of his reign? How long did this festive time last?

c. For whom were the festivities planned?

45

d. According to Esther 1:4, what did the king display to all who came to his festive banquet?

2. Can you think of any big event given by modern-day world leaders that might have a similar motive to that of Ahasuerus? (see Esther 1:4).

3. What was the law of the Persians concerning the drinking of alcohol?

4 a. When you attend a banquet, convention, business meeting or party, have you ever felt a pressure to drink in order to be accepted, or have you experienced an atmosphere like the law of Medes and the Persians?

b. Which attitude do you believe would be the most polite?

(1) Pressuring guests to drink alcoholic beverages in order to be accepted by the group?

(2) Allowing them to make their own choice as King Ahasuerus did?

5. **Challenge:** What do the following Scriptures say concerning alcoholic beverages? Summarize in your own words.

a. Proverbs 23:19-21

b. Proverbs 20:1

6. (Personal) Read Isaiah 28:1 and think of your own nation and its leaders. Do you see any similarities?

SECOND DAY: Read Esther 1:9-22

1. How did Queen Vashti entertain the wives of all the dignitaries from the different provinces?

2. During the final banquet the king gave, which lasted seven days (see Esther 1:3-5), what do you think the king's physical state was, as described in Esther 1:10, and what did he request his servants to do while he was in this condition?

3 a. Since it was not acceptable for a woman to make an appearance at a banquet for men in this pagan culture of Persia, how did Queen Vashti respond to his request?

b. What was the king's emotion when he heard she had refused?

c. What did Memucan say concerning Queen Vashti? Give verse.

4 a. Do you believe that Memucan may have already been a bit henpecked, or simply feared he might have this problem, after reading his statement concerning the queen?

b. What did Memucan propose in Esther 1:19 and what result did he expect it would bring? Briefly summarize. (see Esther 1:20).

5. What did the king say in the letter he sent to all the provinces telling about this new law?

6. (Personal) Just as Queen Vashti is remembered for her stand, is there something special you would like to choose to be remembered for? Are there things you would prefer not to be remembered for? Make a list of each. (see Gal. 5:16-25, if you need some thoughts to help you).

   a. I want to be remembered for:

   b. I would prefer not to be remembered for:

THIRD AND FOURTH DAYS: Since we have read about a pagan culture and a pagan man and wife, and their response to one another, let us pause now and look at some of God's standards for Christian marriage. Read all of Ephesians 5.

1 a. What does Ephesians 5:2 instruct to those who have faith in Christ?

   b. (Personal) Have you invited and received the Lord Jesus Christ into your life so that He can do for you what 1 Peter 2:21-24 describes? Why not stop and pray right now. Invite Him to forgive you and dwell in your life as Savior and Lord.

2   **Challenge:** What are all Christians instructed to do in:

a. Ephesians 5:15

b. Ephesians 5:16

c. Ephesians 5:17

d. Ephesians 5:18

e. Ephesians 5:19

f. Ephesians 5:20

g. Ephesians 5:21

3. What are Christian wives instructed to do in 5:22?

4. Using a dictionary write the meaning of "be subject to" or "be submissive." To find what is meant by these words in the Greek, look up the words *responsive, adaptable* and *regard* in the dictionary.

a. Responsive

b. Adaptable

c. Regard

5. (Personal) Have you had to learn to respond to, adapt to and regard other Christians (see Eph. 5:21)? If you are a wife, have you also had experience in these areas? If possible, share how Christ has especially helped you in some instance.

6 a. How is a Christian husband supposed to love his Christian wife, according to Ephesians 5:25,28?

b. What are the final words on marriage in Ephesians that seem to summarize all of these verses?

FIFTH DAY: Read Proverbs 16:19-33 and Proverbs 23:15-35.

1. From Proverbs 16:19-33, list the characteristics (giving verses) of the wicked man. Then list the characteristics (again giving verses) of the godly man. There will be some verses you may not want to list if they do not sem to fit either category.

a. Wicked man

b. Godly man

2 a. Read Proverbs 16:25 and Romans 6:20-23. What does Romans say is the way that leads to death?

b. Who is able to set us free from sin and death, according to the Romans passage?

c. As we are set from from sin and death, what wonderful gift does God give us, according to Romans 6:22 and 23?

3. Read Proverbs 23:15-35. Imagine you are helping a new Christian, perhaps one of your own children, to understand God's ways. Pick out important verses you would want to stress. Use your own words.

4. **Challenge:** Think back to someone who may have counseled you in one of these ways. Stop and write a letter of thanksgiving to him or her today, or use the telephone to offer your thankfulness. Don't wait until it's too late!

5 a. (Personal) Are you helping someone who needs the good advice found in these Proverbs? As a Christian you should be discipling someone! Pray and ask God to show you that person.

b. Share the verse you memorized. You must know the Bible, if you are going to help others to know it!

SIXTH DAY: Read all of the Notes and look up the Scriptures.

1. What new thought did you find helpful in the Notes?

2. What personal application did you select to apply to your own life this week?

Study Notes

This book is named after its main character, Esther, whose name in Persian means "Star" and in Hebrew, "Myrtle" (Esther 2:7). Although the writer did not use the name of God in this book, God was not to be eliminated from this story! Matthew Henry, the great Bible commentator says, "If the name of God is not here, His finger is." This book demonstrates that God has a part in all of the events of human life.

In Ezra and Nehemiah, the two books preceding Esther, we discover there were many Jewish people who had returned out of captivity to their own land, Israel. Yet there were many who stayed behind in Persia. They did not have the zeal to return to their own land and upset their way of life, which had fallen into a pattern during their captivity by the Babylonians. In the book of Esther we find that even these Jewish people who remained in the provinces of exile were taken care of by God. How wonderfully God used Esther and Mordecai to preserve them.

It is quite certain that the book was written after 465 B.C. for the reign of Xerxes (486-465 B.C.) is spoken of in the past tense (see Esther 10:2). The author also showed the intimate knowledge of the furnishing of the palace in Shushan and of the events of the reign of Xerxes. The author led by God's Spirit was probably a Jewish man who lived in Persia at the time of these narrated events. He no doubt had access to the official chronicle of the kings of Media and Persia (see Esther 2:23; 9:20; 10:2).

A Lesson in History

As we study the history of this period, we discover that Xerxes was the king of Persia, and was called Ahasuerus in the book of Esther. The statement concerning the extent of his rule (see Esther 1:1; 8:9) agrees with the statements of Herodotus's Histories and was true of no other Persian king. Historical scholars agree that Xerxes was none other than the monarch Ahasuerus mentioned in Esther. Thus we may accept this identity as a certainty. Even the feast of the third year of Xerxes reign (see Esther 1:3) harmonizes with the date given by Herodotus for the planning of the Persian king's expedition against Greece. The description of his palace (see Esther 1:6) has been confirmed by its archeological discovery.

As we continue to study, we learn of this king's famous expedition against Greece and how the Greeks defeated his tremendous fleet at the battle of Salamis in 480 B.C. Historians report this is one of the world's most important battles. In parallel passages in Herodotus, we find that the feast described in Esther 1 was the event carefully and majestically planned to bring all of the king's leaders together to plan the campaign against Greece during the third year of his reign.

Hidden Away for God's Purpose

Esther is like Joseph and David in that God had each one hidden away for His purpose. When the day came, He brought them into the forefront to work out His plan. God hid Joseph away in a dungeon in Egypt, but just at the right time, He placed him in the position of prime minister of that country! God always has someone in reserve to fulfill His purposes. Sometimes it's a man like Joseph or Moses. Sometimes it is a woman like Hannah, Esther or Mary. There are many such men and women in history whom God seemed to have prepared and kept for the hour in which He needed them. Just as Esther had "come to royal position for such a time as this" (Esther 4:14), there are times for which God has planned to use you.

> *Just as Esther had "come to royal position for such a time as this" there are times for which God has planned to use you.*

The exact time this story is written and who its author is are not known. The book is placed in time between chapters 6 and 7 of the book of Ezra. Under the edict of King Cyrus, over 50,000 of the Jewish people had returned to their land. Yet there were many who were born in Babylonia, had established themselves in businesses there and were not inclined to cross the desert to begin all over again in Israel, the land of their fathers. If they had all returned to Jerusalem, the book of Esther would not have been written! (see Neh. 2).

The book of Esther demonstrates God's preservation power and His providence for His own people. He not only created the world, He holds it together: "Upholding all things by the word of his power" (Heb. 1:3, *KJV*). "And in him all things hold together" (Col. 1:17,). The world would come unglued today if it were not for God. He is holding together the atoms, the building blocks of this universe. And in God's providence, He directs all things, both good and evil toward a worthy cause—He will have the final victory! "His kingdom ruleth over all" (Ps. 103:19, *KJV*). Yes, God is at the steering wheel of this universe. We need not fear what the ultimate destination is, for with

God in control, we know that all will end well! Shakespeare puts it like this, "There is a divinity that shapes our ends, rough-hew them how we will."

An Example of God's Providence

A perfect example of God's control or providence is the storm that destroyed 300 vessels of Xerxes. This act alone shifted the power from the East to the West, and changed the entire destiny of the world. Xerxes came to Thermopylae and he lost the battle there. Why? He had a superior force, but could only put a few men in that pass. The Greeks had superior soldiers and were masters on the ocean, but they could not match the 300 vessels of Xerxes—but God could. He sent a storm that destroyed all 300 vessels!

Napoleon is quoted as saying that God is on the side of the biggest battalions. But he was wrong because he had the biggest battalions at Waterloo, yet he lost the battle. Again we see God's providence when the Spanish Armada was anchored off the coast of England. The next day England would have gone down in defeat, but that night a storm came. When the morning broke, the Spanish Armada was wrecked. Great Britain, as a result of this, became the leader of the seas for 300 years. Thus the destiny of the world was changed by God.

And so we close this introduction to Esther by saying that none of us know what's around the corner! But be sure, God by His providence is leading. Every day is a new adventure for those who have faith in Jesus Christ. He brings into our lives enemies and trouble, but also gives us His sweetness and love, blessings and abundant life (see John 10:10).

> I cannot be what I am not
> I must work with what I've got
> So for the cause of originality
> I had best, just be me.
>
> The harder I try to be what I'm not
> The sadder becomes my earthly lot.
> All my faults I begin to see
> Lord, I come, just being me.
>
> Oh God I come "Just as I am"
> Knowing for my life you've got a plan
> I'm not all I'd like to be
> But I must present to You,
> Just Plain Me.

Oh God I come as nothing grand
And place my life within your hand
Make me, oh God, the very best me
That by your power I can come to be!
—Donna Pace

A Colossal Celebration Esther 1:1-9

The great feast Vashti refused to come to was held to consider the expedition against Greece, for which Xerxes (Ahasuerus) prepared four years. As this book opens, the king was entertaining all the nobles and princes of his kingdom in the royal palace at Shushan. The banquet was on a colossal scale, lasting 180 days (see Esther 1:4). The men were feasting in the gorgeous palace garden and as was customary the women were entertained separately by Queen Vashti in her private apartment.

Shushan was the winter residence of the Persian kings. Remember that Nehemiah was in the palace in Shushan (see Neh. 1:1). Loftus excavated and identified this palace in 1852, and in 1884 Dieulafay continued the excavation. The Frenchman in 1884 definitely located the places mentioned in the book of Esther—the "inner court," the "outer court," the "king's gate," the "palace garden." He even found a die or "pur" they used to cast lots.

As the scene opens we have this great social event in progress with even the color scheme outlined for us (see Esther 1:6,7). Perhaps one of the most extravagant parties since that time was the one hosted by the Shah of Iran (Iran was ancient Persia). *Time* magazine in October 1971 covered this great banquet and estimated the cost to be $100,000. The Shah's guest list included 9 kings, 5 queens, 13 princes, 8 princesses and 16 presidents. The occasion for this great celebration was the twenty-fifth hundred year anniversary of the founding of the Persian Empire by Cyrus the Great.

We do not know the cost of the banquet given in Esther chapter 1, but we do discover that the kings and the princes were in the midst of their drunken revelry (see Esther 1:10). The phrase "the king was merry with wine" probably indicates he was not himself when he ordered that Queen Vashti be brought before the guests to display her beauty (see Esther 1:11). According to custom, no Persian woman would do this, for it would be an insult to her womanhood. We know Vashti must have been attractive, for her name in the Persian language means "beautiful woman."

Imagine the repercussions when Vashti refused to return with the men the king had sent to bring her to his banquet! Undoubtedly the king had announced the imminent arrival of his beautiful queen. All of the men were awaiting her royal beauty. What a sight for them all to enjoy and the king to glory in! And now the messengers return with her refusal to appear (see Esther 1:10-12). In the Eastern cultures of that day, women, even if they were the queen of a realm, had no right to make such a choice, for they were considered inferior and only a possession to be owned.

Jesus—Woman's Best Friend

Perhaps we should stop and think of the benefits Christianity has brought to womanhood. In a special sense, Jesus Christ is woman's best friend. Feminine leadership in Old Testament times, though it was limited by custom, was blessed by God. Deborah, for example, was a leader (see Judg. 4).

Scripture speaks of prophecy as a gift from God, and declares emphatically that this gift is given to women as well as to men. And in the New Testament, in Acts 21:9, we are told the evangelist Philip had four daughters who prophesied.

Man and woman have by nature been created by God with different physical and psychological needs. Thus, each are intended to complement each other in society.

The Lord Jesus Christ Himself welcomed the presence of women among His disciples (see Luke 8:1-3). He used the opportunity to transform the woman of Samaria, an adulteress and prostitute, into an effective evangelist (see John 4:27-30). He rejoiced over Mary's choice of occupation (see Luke 10:42) as opposed to Martha's insistence that her sister stick completely to traditional female duties. The prophetess Anna did not keep silence in the church but became one of the first to speak of Christ's coming! (see Luke 2:36-38).

A New Identity in Christ

The Christian woman has been given a new identity in Christ (see Gal. 3:28). She shares with the Christian man the calling of a ministry of reconciliation to God. She is valued as a responsible member of the body of Christ. God endows her with His gifts for the building up of the believers (see 1 Cor. 12:7). The same power of the Holy Spirit is available to the woman as to the man, enabling her to fulfill her ministry in her home, her church and her world. In Jesus Christ woman truly discovers the abundant life (see John 10:10). Not only a woman's spiritual life, but all her life experiences become transformed when she knows Jesus Christ as her personal Lord and Savior.

Nowhere in the Bible will you find male superiority or female inferiority taught. What the Bible teaches is the indispensability under God of man and woman, both in society and the sphere of the home. Woman was made from man (see 1 Cor. 11:8) and is not inferior, but indispensable to the completeness of humanity (see Gen. 2:20-23). Man and woman have by nature been created by God with different physical and psychological needs. Thus, each are intended to complement each other in society, and within the sanctity of the Christian marriage relationship, which is planned for some men and women by God (see Gen. 2:24).

Love as Christ Loves the Church

Man, as head of a Christian home, has God in authority over him. The wife acknowledges she is not the head of the home, but that she is responsible to the earthly head, her husband, and is also equally accountable to God. "Each one of you also must love his wife as he loves himself, and the wife must respect her husband" (Eph. 5:33).

The husband in turn is responsible to love his wife, cherish and care for her "as Christ loved the church and gave himself up for her to make her holy, cleansing her by the washing with water through the word, and to present her to himself as a radiant church, without stain or wrinkle or any other blemish, but holy and blameless. In the same way, husbands ought to love their wives as their own bodies. He who loves his wife loves himself. After all, no one ever hated his own body, but he feeds and cares for it, just as Christ does the church—for we are members of his body" (Eph. 5:25-30).

Submission of wives to their husbands is to be "fitting in the Lord" (Col. 3:18), while the husbands are instructed to "love your wives and do not be harsh with them" (Col. 3:19). This means that no man should try to subject a wife to his domination while he neglects God's dominion, guidance and wisdom in his own life. The Christian man becomes a responsible authoritative head in his home when he submits his life and will to the Lord Jesus Christ. The Christian woman must also submit her life and will to the Lord Jesus Christ to become a responsible "helpmate" to her husband. By this submission of their lives to Christ the Lord, the couple then experiences God's promise in Romans 5:5: "The love of God is shed abroad in our hearts by the Holy Ghost which is given unto us" (*KJV*).

What About the Non-Christian Spouse?

But what about the person who is married to a non-Christian? What is their attitude to be? The Bible says, "Wives, in the same way be submissive to your husbands so that, if any of them do not believe the word, they may be won over without talk by the behavior of their wives, when they see the purity and reverence of your lives" (1 Pet. 3:1,2).

In most cases it is completely possible for the wife to lovingly cherish, honor and obey her non-Christian husband, and for the Christian husband to cherish and honor his non-Christian wife. However, at times there are extreme circumstances when a person might be asked to violate their Christian conscience, and it is at this point that the Christian partner must gently, lovingly, but obediently "obey God rather than men" (Acts 5:29).

A King Calls for His Queen Esther 1:10-12

There were probably one to two thousand people gathered at this banquet, for they had come from 127 provinces to be with the king. Imagine the cost of food and lodging for these guests for 180 days (see Esther 1:1-4).

As a climax to all this entertainment, the king made a feast in the court gardens for seven more days (see Esther 1:5). This banquet ended up in what appears to be a drunken orgy, although no one was compelled to drink according to the law of that day (see Esther 1:8). These Oriental rulers never forced anyone to drink though they themselves often "overindulged" (see Esther 1:10), which was "to be merry with wine."

Perhaps the king did not want to embarrass his queen, whom he loved very much, by bringing her before a group of drunken men to display her beauty. Yet in his "merry" state, as described in Esther 1:10, the king made a decision that he would not have made under normal circumstances, for it would not have been proper for the queen to appear at the men's banquet.

The queen refused to appear before the king at the end of the feast, however, which must have broken up the party abruptly. It was sad that the drunken king had sent for his beloved queen to present her to his associates, many of whom were probably in the same condition. She was to wear her royal crown and display her beauty (see Esther 1:10,11).

It was a shame that he chose to expose the modesty of his wife Vashti, who was dining separately with the women in another area according to the Persian custom.

Is Disobedience Justified?

Yet, perhaps Vashti did not use wisdom in denying him his wish. There are many different attitudes expressed by Bible scholars on her response to the request. Matthew Henry says, "She refused to come though he sent his command by seven honourable messengers, and publicly. Josephus (the historian) says the king sent for her again and again, yet she persisted in her denial. Had she come, while it was evident that she did it in pure obedience, it would have been no reflection upon her modesty, nor a bad example. Perhaps she refused in a haughty manner, and then it was certainly evil; she scorned to come at the king's commandment" (p. 1124, Matthew Henry's Commentary).

Other Bible scholars feel that because Vashti was a pagan queen, she acted according to her inward conscience as given by God in her refusal to be put on a vulgar display before drunken men. J. Vernon McGee in his book, *Esther, The Romance of Providence* states, "According to the etiquette of that day, she did not belong there . . . . There is no law that could make her come; she stood and said she would not." We must remember that this was an experience in a pagan monarchy where there was no worship of the true and living God.

Demise of a Queen Esther 1:13-22

Because Vashti refused to appear before the king, he retaliated by deposing the queen. Memucan is very concerned about Vashti's refusal to appear at the banquet and says, "Queen Vashti has wronged not only the king, but every official and citizen of your empire. For women everywhere will begin to disobey their husbands when they learn what Queen Vashti has done. And before this day is out the wife of everyone of us officials throughout your empire will hear what the queen did and will start talking to us husbands the same way, and there will be contempt and anger throughout your realm." He was probably right too! Wives probably would have begun to disobey and domineer their husbands!

What Can a Christian Wife Expect?

How different the situation should be in a Christian marriage! God never wants a Christian husband to issue a directive a Christian wife would find vulgar, against God's will, and thus impossible to obey. As the wife submits herself to her Spirit-filled husband—responsively, with consideration and respect—she has a right to expect that her

59

husband will humbly love her as much as Christ loves the church (see Eph. 5:15-33) and not ask of her anything that would not be pleasing to God. There would be much heartache removed in many marriages if these principles were remembered by both partners.

This pagan law revealed the character of Xerxes as he stood in history. Here he agreed to a man's law that could not be changed in any way or revoked (see Esther 1:21,22). In his unreasonable anger the king allowed this banishment of his lovely queen. It became the law of the Medes and the Persians. Later the king wanted to break the law because he loved Vashti, but he could not.

This experience must have been hard for the queen—it cost her her throne, the love of her husband and perhaps her very existence. Yet in God's providence she had an important place in furthering God's plan for His own people, the children of Israel. Yes, God's providence served its own purpose through these events, which made way for Esther to receive the crown and become queen.

Are You Available for God's Use?

To work out His plans, God used people. How do you believe God wants to use you this week to work out His plan in your life, in your circumstances, and in your community? Are you willing to allow Him the freedom to use your life every day, every hour, every minute of this week? Will you allow Him to show you the needs of the people around you, the needs of your family, the needs of your friends? Trust Him to work through you by the power of His Holy Spirit to bring about His plan this week for you in His world (see Zech. 4:6).

PRIORITIES

Lord, show me your priorities
   for me
      today
         tomorrow
            and always.

What were your priorities when you walked
   this earth?
      To glorify God
         and to be obedient to your Father's will.

What were Paul's priorities, Lord?
      Philippians 1:20—"According to my earnest expectation and my hope, that in nothing I shall be ashamed, but that with all boldness, as always, so now also *Christ shall be* magnified in my body, whether it be by life, or by death."

60

And what did James say, Lord?
James 4:14,15—"Our life is but a vapour,
that appeareth for a little time,
and then vanisheth away.
For that ye ought to say,
If the Lord will,
we shall live,
and do this, or that."

And what did you tell Peter, Lord?
Who had denied you thrice
What were his priorities to be?
"Feed my lambs, feed my sheep."

And Jesus said to Peter in Luke 22:32
"But I have prayed for thee
that thy faith fail not:
and when thou art converted,
strengthen thy brethren."
Please Lord, *show me my priorities.*

       —Doris Greig

A New Queen Is Chosen

ESTHER 2 AND 3

Before you begin you study this week:
1. Pray and ask God to speak to you through His Holy Spirit each day.
2. Use only your Bible for your answers.
3. Write your answers and the verses you have used.
4. Challenge questions are for those who have the time and wish to do them.
5. Personal questions are to be shared with your study group only if you wish to share.
6. As you study look for a verse to memorize this week. Write it down, carry it with you, tack it to your bulletin board, tape it to the dashboard of your car. Make a real effort to learn the verse and its reference.

FIRST DAY: Read all of Esther 2 concentrating on verses 1-10.

1. When the king's servants recognized how much the king missed Queen Vashti, what plan did they make to find a new queen? Briefly summarize Esther 2:1-4.

2 a. What was the name of the Jewish man who adopted Esther, and why did he adopt her?

b. How is Esther described?

   c. When Mordecai brought Esther to the palace, what did Hegai, the keeper of the women, do for Esther?

3. Why didn't Esther tell Hegai that she was Jewish?

4 a. **Challenge:** We can only wonder what Esther's emotions were as she responded obediently to Mordecai and went to live in the palace. Today Christians are fortunate to have verses of encouragement and special guidance they can rely upon when they question their difficult circumstances. Put the following verses into your own words or insert your name into them to make them personal promises from God to you.

   Psalm 32:8

   Isaiah 58:11

   John 16:13

   b. (Personal) Which of these verses was the most encouraging in your present situation? Why? If possible share with your discussion group.

5 a. (Personal) Esther was put in an unusual place by God, yet she knew instinctively that she should obey both her cousin and Hegai, the keeper of the women. What about you? Are you in a place of service where you are sure God has placed you— perhaps in a choir, teaching in a Sunday School, leading a Bible class or some other area of Christian work? Even though others may criticize you for your obedience to God, and feel you should be doing something else, or suggest that you should involve yourself in more activities than you have strength for, are you

willing to stand firm and do what you know God has asked you to do? Give an example without names.

b. What does Peter say in Acts 5:29 that could help you as you pray and make decisions concerning the place where God would have you serve Him?

6 a. (Personal) What do you think were some of Esther's attitudes that pleased Hegai? (see Esther 2:8,9). Think about how good attitudes like thoughtfulness, kindness, cheerfulness, helpfulness, understanding and humbleness could be used to further your outreach for Christ in your business, home, neighborhood or community. List the attitudes you want to pray about and ask God to change in your life this week (see Gal. 5:22).

b. (Personal) What encouragement do you find in Psalm 42:8,11 concerning your attitudes?

SECOND DAY: Read Esther 2:11-20.

1. Who walked every day before the women's court? What do you think he did for Esther as he walked there? (Use your imagination as you read Esther 2:11.)

2 a. As Christians, we need to take time to care and pray for those in need as well as pray for ourselves. Often we kneel, but at what other times and in what other places than our homes can we pray?

b. (Personal) Can you think of an example of an answered prayer that has been "sent up" as you walked, talked or sat in some particular spot?

3 a. **Challenge:** The following verses concern prayer. Write them out in your own words or use the words in your Bible, but be sure to add your own name to the prayer promise.

Psalm 17:6-8

Psalm 38:15

Isaiah 58:9

b. (Personal) Which of these verses challenged you to "pray without ceasing" or helped you in some other area concerning prayer to God? (see 1 Thess. 5:17).

4. a. How long were the women, in the care of Hegai, given a "beauty treatment" before they saw the king? (see Esther 2:12).

b. What was the king's impression when he saw Esther? Give verse.

5. a. Though we recognize that all of these events were God's plan to eventually save the Jewish people from extermination, let us look at this event in the light of today's society. Do you believe people today judge each other more by physical appearance than personal integrity and character? Do husbands ever

choose their wives by the standards this pagan king used long ago? If so, can you as a Christian friend or parent change this wrong attitude by training the future generation to judge people by God's standards? How?

b. How would Proverbs 31:30 and Ezekiel 16:14 help you explain this to someone?

6. How was Esther obedient to Mordecai in Esther 2:20?

THIRD DAY: Read Esther 2:21-23.

1. How did Mordecai save the king's life? (see Esther 2:21-23).

2. (Personal) Mordecai saw a special need. The king's life was in danger. He responded to that need and saved the king's life. Analyze your life and the needs of your family, neighborhood and church. Is there a need for special service in one of these areas? Evaluate the qualities God has given you. Pray and ask God how He wants to use you this week. List some of the qualities God has given to you, thanking Him for each one.

a. How can I help family or friends?

b. How can I help my neighborhood or community?

c. How can I help my church?

3. Mordecai had not revealed to the king his relationship as adoptive father to Queen Esther. When he heard that two men

plotted to kill the king he could have decided it would be safer not to get involved. Yet he did not choose this route. He involved himself to the point that the king now knew his name (see Esther 2:22). What about society today? Do you feel most people are concerned about the welfare of others? Can you think of instances where people have shown real concern for others, and other times when they have not? Share from your own experiences.

4. **Challenge:** Read Luke 10:30-37. Who did not demonstrate concern in this story? Who illustrated concern and therefore was called the "neighbor" of the bandit's victim?

5. (Personal) Can you pinpoint some time and place in your life when you were at the right place at the right time and with God's help responded to a need? Share your experiences to encourage others to see God's plan for their lives in times such as these.

6 a. What does Ephesians 2:8,9 tell you about faith in Jesus Christ as Savior and Lord?

   b. **Challenge:** Read James 2:14-20. How can people see that a person has faith in the Lord Jesus Christ? (see also James 1:22).

FOURTH DAY: Read all of Esther 3 concentrating on verses 1-6.

1 a. Who was promoted by the king and how was he respected by the king's servants?

   b. Who refused to bow down and give reverence to Haman?

c. According to Esther 3:4, what had Mordecai told these men who asked him why he wouldn't bow before Haman?

2. What were Haman's emotions toward Mordecai and how did he seek revenge? Give verses.

3. (Personal) Mordecai was willing to risk suffering rather than bow down and worship a man, Haman. He only bowed to the true and living God. Most of us know nothing of suffering for the sake of Christ. How willing do you think you would be to stand up boldly, kindly and openly confess your faith in the Lord Jesus Christ before unbelievers? Are you willing to be different if the Holy Spirit leads you to take a stand?

4. Read Psalm 37. List numbers of verses that could apply to Haman's attitude toward Mordecai. Write down one of the verses that particularly impresses you and give its reference.

5. Reread Psalm 37 and list all of the verses by reference number where you find God's promises to those who trust in Him. Write down one or two verses that are especially meaningful to you for your life experiences this week.

FIFTH DAY: Read Esther 3:7-15.

1. What reasons did Haman give to the king to convince him the Jewish people in his realm should be destroyed? Give verse.

2. What did Haman request from the king in Esther 3:9?

69

3. How did the king respond to Haman's request and how did he confirm his response?

4 a. To initiate the killing of the Jews, scribes were called in to write letters telling of these orders. To whom were these letters sent?

b. Whose name and seal was put on these letters?

5 a. Have there been other rulers in later generations who tried to exterminate the Jewish race?

b. Do you see God's hand preserving this race of people throughout history? Many have suffered, but still the Jewish people are a distinct race. Read Genesis 12:1-3 and write your thoughts about God's blessings promised here.

6. Did you memorize a verse from the Bible this week? Share the verse and how you memorized it. This will encourage others to memorize God's Word too.

SIXTH DAY: Read all of the Notes and look up all of the Scriptures.

1. What new thought did you find helpful in the Notes?

2. What personal application did you select to apply to your own life this week?

Study Notes

This chapter begins with the phrase "after these events." We discover that the king's anger had eased and he remembered his lovely queen, Vashti. But he knew the decree to dethrone her was a law that could not be reversed according to the law of the Medes and Persians (see Esther 1:19).

Certainly the men who had suggested she be dethroned must have feared the king might defy this law and bring back Vashti to reign as queen again. It would have spelled death for those men who had plotted against her. These men had suggested to the king, in Esther 1:19-22, that Vashti be removed from her royal throne as an example to all the women in the land of the terrible punishment disobedience to a husband in the realm of Persia would bring. The sad results of her disobedience was to be an everlasting reminder to the wives of all men in the Mede and Persian Empire.

When the leaders of the country saw that King Ahasuerus (Xerxes) longed for Vashti again, they immediately proposed a new queen be chosen from among the most beautiful virgins in the land. They demonstrated their awareness of the terrible danger that could come their way if Vashti returned, by being willing to waive the custom of choosing the queen from among one of their own family. They were even willing to take a foreign queen!

Actually between chapters 1 and 2, history records that Ahasuerus made his historic attack on Greece with an army of 5 million men and suffered a terrible defeat. Therefore, not only had he lost his beloved queen, but he had suffered a great military defeat, as well. Josephus, the historian, said that when King Ahasuerus's anger toward Vashti was over, he was exceedingly grieved that the matter was carried so far, and would have been reconciled, but that, by the constitution of the government, the judgment was irrevocable.

All the provinces of his kingdom were searched for fair young virgins; officers were even appointed by the king to search all the provinces for the loveliest ladies (see Esther 2:2,3). A special house called "a seraglio" was prepared for those chosen, and Hegai, the king's chamberlain, was appointed to be in charge. The women brought into the seraglio would undergo a process of purification for 12 months, under the supervision of Hegai. Then from among all these maidens the king would choose the one to replace Vashti as queen. This plan was presented to the king, and because it pleased him, he agreed to all of it (see Esther 2:4).

Unlikely Candidate for Queen Esther 2:5-11

The most beautiful girls in the 127 provinces of the king's empire had been gathered together in the women's quarters of the king's palace. No beauty contest like this had ever been held before and no beauty queen had ever had such a prize dangled before her—a crown! The girl who was chosen would not be "queen for a day," but would wear the royal crown and be the queen of a proud empire. There must have been hundreds of girls brought by the officials to Shushan. The only judge of this contest was to be the king himself!

Now in the capital of Shushan, or "Susa," there was a certain Jew named Mordecai who was a Benjamite. We now find the true hero and heroine of this book being introduced. Mordecai was the great grandson of a man named Kish, who had been carried off to Babylon with King Jeconiah in 597 B.C. When Mordecai's uncle, Abihail, (see Esther 2:15) died, Esther was adopted into Mordecai's home. Since she had neither father nor mother, Mordecai raised her as his own daughter (see Esther 2:7).

When the announcement was made that there was to be chosen another queen for the king, Mordecai immediately became interested. He took his young cousin, Esther, and entered her into the beauty contest. Now we see the providence of God moving into this situation, for we read in Esther 2:9, "the girl pleased" Hegai, the keeper of the women. It was no accident that she obtained kindness from him, for undoubtedly she had a pleasant personality and a good attitude, which God in His providence had given her along with her beauty. God had a purpose for her life and had given her certain attributes to bring about this purpose.

Mordecai came into the life of Esther on the basis of adoption (see Esther 2:7). She was obedient to him and allowed him to take her to the king's palace for this great contest. She did not reveal her identity as a Jewess, at her uncle's request (see Esther 2:10). Mordecai took on the responsibility to educate and care for Esther, guiding her steps and her divine destiny. We too are to obey the Holy Spirit's leading, just as Esther obeyed her uncle, Mordecai. "For as many as are led by the Spirit of God, they are the sons of God. For ye have not received the spirit of bondage again to fear; but ye have received the Spirit of adoption, whereby we cry, Abba, Father" (Rom. 8:14,15, KJV).

Holy Spirit—the Spirit of Adoption

The Holy Spirit is the Spirit of adoption! When a person is born into the family of God and becomes His child (see John 3), it is the presence of the Holy Spirit within that person that is a seal God sets upon the new relationship. In the relationship that existed between Mordecai and Esther, we have a beautiful picture of the relationship that exists between the Holy Spirit and those who by faith have received Him. The faith through which we receive the Holy Spirit is the same faith through which we claim redemption and forgiveness through the blood of the Lord Jesus Christ. "Not by works of righteousness which we have done, but according to his mercy he saved us, by the washing of regeneration, and renewing of the Holy Ghost; which he shed on us abundantly through Jesus Christ our Saviour" (Titus 3:5, 6, *KJV*).

Have you received the Lord Jesus Christ as your Lord and Savior? If so, then the Holy Spirit, as these Scriptures have said, has come to take residence within your human spirit. You have been born again and God has set His seal upon you as His child. If you have not made the decision to receive the Lord Jesus Christ into your life yet, stop now and read John chapter 3 and Revelation 3:20! (see also Eph. 1:7, 13, 14).

In the Right Place at the Right Time

In Esther 2:11 we discover that Mordecai walked every day before the court of the women's house, to know how Esther acted, and what should become of her. God had His Mordecai in the right place at the right time. Neither captivity nor exile from his homeland changed Mordecai's loyalty to his Jewish destiny. His position in the palace is not specified, but it is clear that he must have had some political appointments, for we read that he was within the palace household. Otherwise he would not have been able to walk before the women's household and check on Esther's welfare.

Certainly Esther must have felt lonely in her place of destiny. She must have wondered how she would be treated by the other women in the king's harem. It must have been difficult to have been plucked from her own environment and planted in the king's palace with so many beautiful girls. Yet she was obedient to Mordecai, who must have assured her that he felt this was the right thing to do and that he would always stand watch over her. Christians can be assured that when they are obedient to the Lord Jesus Christ, He too will always be standing watch over them.

An Almost Impossible Situation

Esther's situation seemed almost impossible. There were hundreds of pretty girls from all over the empire. Everyone was asking, "Will they ever find one as lovely as Vashti?" Yet God always acts in impossible situations! What is your impossible situation? "When God acts in an impossible situation, He becomes greater to us. The more impossible the situation, the more honor is given to Him. Therefore, in spite of prevailing prayer, He often waits until the last minute before He intervenes. Thus He teaches us to 'hold on in faith.'" (A quote from M. Basilea Schlink.)

A New Queen Is Chosen Esther 2:12-18

Let's take a look at the scene of this palace where Esther had been residing for one year. Archeologists have found that the foundation of the palace was a platform 50 feet high, covering an area of two and a half acres. Underneath this platform was a vast sewer system many miles long through which a visitor may walk today. The walls of this palace were covered with the most magnificent carvings, reliefs and inscriptions.

We know this is so because two large rooms with these art pieces are on display in the Louvre Museum in France today. While excavating, these carvings were found preserved as fresh and beautiful as they were when Queen Esther looked upon them. In Esther 1:5-7 we find a brief description of the palace with its richly colored awnings stretched across the marble pillars to silver rods. These awnings shaded the guests as they reclined on gold and silver seats, feasting and drinking day after day (see Esther 1:5-8).

The city itself, where this great palace of Ahasuerus stood, was destroyed by fire in 331 B.C. by Alexander the Great. It has been buried in the sand of the desert ever since. In 1930 the Oriental Institute of Chicago received permission from the Persian government to excavate and restore the palace as completely as possible. For this reason we know the magnificent glory and beauty with which Esther was surrounded during her reign as Queen of Persia.

Two years after Ahasuerus made his historic attack on Greece, suffering a terrible defeat, he married Esther. She was his queen for 13 years. Esther no doubt lived for many years into the reign of her stepson, Artaxerxes. It was under his reign that Nehemiah rebuilt Jerusalem.

In Esther 2:12-14 we read of how a king in that day chose his queen. Some suggest Esther committed a great sin when she entered the king's chamber to present herself as a candidate for his queen. We must consider that everyone the king took to his bed was married to him, for the king had many wives. Yet he would have only one queen. Remember this was a pagan court and a pagan law that had nothing to do with the Mosaic Law.

God Frequently Overrules Man's Laws

Yet God overruled. Notice, "Now when the turn of Esther, the daughter of Abihail the uncle of Mordecai, who had taken her for his daughter, was come to go in unto the king, she required nothing but what Hegai, the king's chamberlain, the keeper of the women, appointed" (Esther 2:15, *KJV*). We can only speculate on her feelings, but we read in this passage that she asked for nothing, other than what Hegai advised.

Esther revealed a unique spirit when she was to appear before the king by not asking for special garments or jewelry with which to adorn herself. She did not seem to be concerned in pleasing the king by "outward adorning of plaiting the hair, and of wearing of gold, or of putting on of apparel." Instead her ornament was "a meek and quiet spirit which is in the sight of God of great price" (1 Pet. 3:3,4, *KJV*). It is not surprising that she was chosen by the providence of God to be the queen. Yes! God had a purpose for her life, and this was the first step in fulfillment of that purpose.

How Do You Spend Your Time?

What about you? Where has God placed you? How are you spending the time God has given you? Whether your name is Billy Graham, or you're the president of some great country, or just John Doe, each one of you receives an equal allotment of time: 168 hours a week. The difference is how you spend those hours. None of us would throw away bits of money, but all of us are guilty of throwing away our time and influence. In two minutes you could write down an all-inclusive list of your lifetime goals—personal, family, career, financial and spiritual. Amazingly enough, in the same length of time you could answer the question, "How would I like to spend the next four years?" We need to define our goals, both short- and long-range.

As we abide and trust in the Lord Jesus Christ, He will help us plan our time and our years.

The University of Wisconsin discovered through an interesting study that the typical person spends three years in the course of his lifetime just waiting! According to a Gallup poll out of 100 people selected at random, all of them expected to do some waiting in the next few hours, yet only one in eight had any plans to use their waiting time constructively!

75

A Christian can always have a Bible, a good book or a tape at hand to listen to while waiting. You can carry a small box with your correspondence and use your waiting time effectively to write to those who need to hear from you! We can transform spaces of time into fruitful seasons of harvest! The hour on the plane next to a spiritually needy person can be valuable throughout all eternity. The moment spent waiting for the attendant to refuel your car can be prayerfully given to God.

Circumstances May Vary, but Amount of Time Does Not

Every life is different with many different circumstances, but we all have time. We need to remember, "I am the vine, ye are the branches. He that abideth in me, and I in him, the same bringeth forth much fruit: for without me ye can do nothing" (John 15:5, *KJV*). As we abide and trust in the Lord Jesus Christ, He will help us plan our time and our years. This means that we must spend time in prayer to our Lord asking Him to guide us!

In the month of December 479 B.C., just four years after his divorce from Vashti, Xerxes (Ahasuerus) set the royal crown upon Esther's head and made her his queen (see Esther 2:17). Her reign began as the deposed Vashti's had ended—with a banquet. Esther was the honored guest and the king charitably granted remission of taxes to the provinces and gave gifts with royal liberality in honor of Queen Esther.

A Contrast in the Treatment of Women

As we reflect on the impact Christianity has had on our culture today, we see the contrast between the way women were treated then and now. I'm sure every woman reading the book of Esther feels glad to live in a culture where she has a choice and her feelings are considered in the important matters of marriage. Yet there are many lands today where there are still arrangements made by heads of state or by parents for young girls to marry, without freedom of choice. These lands are lands where Christianity has not had an impact. It was really Christ who brought to women a new prestige.

With all the new freedom and honor Christ brought to women, He also gave responsibility. Woman's primary role remains that of wife, mother and homemaker. "Teach the young women to be sober, to love their husbands, to love their children, to be discreet, chaste, keepers at home, good, obedient to their own husbands, that the word of God be not blasphemed" (Titus 2:4,5, *KJV*).

76

I believe the Bible teaches that women have been freed by Jesus Christ, and have been given a noble, God-given role to obey God's laws. And I believe a woman who loves God will want to remain feminine and be what she is meant to be. She need not neglect her community responsibilities, for Christ would not expect this of a woman! Christ in His mercy and justice would want women to receive an equal wage if they find it necessary to work to earn their living.

The Lord Jesus Christ has freed woman to be what God created her to be. She has identity and purpose. She needs to seek God's perfect will for her life and follow it obediently. "Honor goes to kind and gracious women" (Prov. 11:16, *TLB*). "I plead with you to give your bodies to God. Let them be a living sacrifice, holy—the kind he can accept. When you think of what he has done for you, is this too much to ask? Don't copy the behavior and customs of this world, but be a new and different person with a fresh newness in all you do and think. Then you will learn from your own experience how his ways will really satisfy you" (Rom. 12:1,2, *TLB*).

The Best Laid Plans . . . Esther 2:19-23

It's difficult to understand in the light of our culture why the virgins were gathered together for the second time in Esther 2:19. It was during this second gathering that Mordecai discovered the plot against the life of the king. We find in Esther 2:19 that Mordecai was sitting at the king's gate. How did he get there? By the providence of God! The details are not given of how Mordecai had gotten into politics. Sitting in the king's gate meant that he had a new position as a judge, for the courthouse in the ancient world was the gate of the city.

As Mordecai sat in the king's gate, two of the king's chamberlains, Bigthana and Teresh, who kept the door, were angry and decided to kill the king. Mordecai in his new position overheard this plot and told Esther about it. Naturally Esther told the king (see Esther 2:22). The king undoubtedly put his "F.B.I." into action to check it out! (see Esther 2:23). The king's secret investigation proved Mordecai's statement to be true and the men plotting against his life were hanged from the gallows. We find this incident was recorded in the book of the chronicles in the presence of the king (see Esther 2:23).

We do not read of Mordecai being rewarded for what he had done. This is an important fact and we will discover later there was a very special reason why he was not rewarded at this time. Mordecai may have brooded over this many times and wondered why he had been ignored and not honored for what he had discovered. But again, it was the providence of God.

There may have been things that have happened in all our lives for

77

which we feel we have not been rewarded. One day in God's providence we shall see God turning what has happened in the past into
blessings for His glory in the future. If you are in a hard place today,
remember that God will use your faithfulness in some way. Remember that God has not taken His hand off this earth nor off you, no matter what is happening. Whoever you are, God is moving in your life.
Trust Him as your Savior and your Guide, and you will be able to look
back over your life and see His providence worked out through all
your experiences.

One Man's Courage Esther 3:1-6

Now we see the form of Haman casting a shadow across our picture.
Mordecai refuses to bow before Haman after Xerxes has elevated
Haman to the second highest position in the kingdom. Haman was a
wicked man whose day of triumph was short and whose joy endured
but for a moment (see Job 20:4,5). Haman's wrath was aroused
against Mordecai's nation when he would not bow to him (see Esther
3:2).

Mordecai was honest when he was asked why he would not obey
the king's command and confessed that he was a Jew (see Esther
3:4). Haman, swelled with pride, was bitterly humiliated that this man
would not bow before him. He determined that Mordecai and every
Jewish person in the kingdom would die (see Esther 3:6).

This decree of Haman's was to go out into all the provinces, which
meant that the Jews scattered throughout the Media-Persian Empire,
covering two continents including Europe, would be killed.

As Mordecai began to stand out as a man of God, we see Haman
beginning to stand out in all his ugliness as a man for the devil. Haman
attempted to destroy all of the Jewish people. He did not know anything about the promise that God made to Abraham: "And I will make
of thee a great nation, and I will bless thee, and make thy name great;
and thou shalt be a blessing: and I shall bless them that bless thee,
and curse him that curseth thee: and in thee shall all families of the
earth be blessed" (Gen. 12:2,3, *KJV*).

Throughout the ages God has kept His Word. He has preserved
these people as we will see in the book of Esther.

A Plot to Destroy God's People Esther 3:7-15

Haman cast lots to determine the day his enemies would be
destroyed (see Esther 3:7). Haman tried to prove to the king that all
the Jews were disloyal subjects (see Esther 3:8). Haman offered to
pay the king a $20 million bribe to see to it that the Jews were killed!

78

(see Esther 3:9). The king signed a royal decree, which meant that every man, woman and child who were Jews would be killed and all their property would be taken. Letters were sent to all the provinces that these people were to be destroyed at this time (see Esther 3:13). Imagine the fasting, praying, weeping and sadness that took place among the Jews at this time.

"But the city Shushan was perplexed" (Esther 3:15, *KJV*). The king and Haman sat down to drink after they had sent out the decree to all of the provinces. But the people in the city couldn't understand all of this. Though they considered the Jewish people foreigners with different customs, they didn't want to kill them. These Jewish captives had made many friends in their captivity. Undoubtedly the grief of the doomed people was shared with many of the Medes and Persians.

We too could join in the despair of such a story except that we know the end of it! God's providence was at work. He had a plan for a Jewish woman to one day be the mother of the Savior of all mankind. The Jews must survive! The Jewish race will survive until God winds up His clock for the last time (see Jer. 31:35,36).

God Watches over His Own

God stands in the shadow keeping watch over His own. Today there are Christian believers throughout the whole wide world who are being persecuted as these Jewish people were in the Media-Persian Empire. Here is what one Red Army war veteran wrote after more than eight years without trial in a Stalinist labor camp: "People are tired of atheistic propaganda. Books on atheism lie in piles unsold in the book stores, but I think we all know what scenes there would be if they ever put Bibles on sale! Young people keep asking me, 'Where can I get a Bible?' There just aren't any . . . . In old Russia you could get all the books you wanted, churches were open, but faith was not so deep. In the West they have all these things, all they want, but religion is still only a superficial thing there. Here we have nothing, but religion is growing stronger and stronger. It is only strong when it must bear a cross."

If you are suffering any form of persecution today because of your faith in the Lord Jesus Christ, thank God for it. It will only make you grow stronger and help you to be a more loving and persuasive witness for the Lord Jesus Christ. Remember, God has His hand upon you and His providence is at work in your life, just as it was long ago in the life of Esther and Mordecai (see Heb. 13:8).

FOR SUCH A TIME AS THIS

ESTHER 4 AND 5

Before you begin your study this week:
1. Pray and ask God to speak to you through His Holy Spirit each day.
2. Use only your Bible for your answers.
3. Write down your answers and the verses you have used.
4. Challenge questions are for those who have the time and wish to do them.
5. Personal questions are to be shared with your study group only if you wish to share.
6. As you study look for a verse to memorize this week. Write it down, carry it with you, tack it to your bulletin board, tape it to the dashboard of your car. Make a real effort to learn the verse and its reference.

FIRST DAY: Read all of Esther 4 concentrating on verses 1-8.

1. What did Mordecai do after he heard about the decree the king had signed and sent to all of his provinces? (see Esther 3:13). Read Esther 4:1,2.

2. **Challenge:** Why do you think Queen Esther sent out new clothes for her Uncle Mordecai to put on? (see Esther 4:4). Did she send him a "new suit" because she wanted to see him and knew that traditionally no person could enter the king's "royal gate" and appear in the palace area dressed in sackcloth and ashes? Or, did she send him a new suit because some of the materialism of

81

living as a queen in a king's palace had influenced her to feel that her relative should not be wearing such clothes? What do you think her motives were?

3. (Personal) What is the motive behind your life-style—such as the way you dress, the decoration of your home, your choice of friends, the way you present your personality to the world at large? Who are you trying to please or impress, man or God?

4. **Challenge:** Read Psalm 145:1-5 and Psalm 138. Choose at least four verses that remind you to praise God for His love and help in your life each day.

5. When Mordecai refused to change his suit (see Esther 4:4), how did Esther find out about the edict the king had signed to destroy all of the Jews?

6. What did Mordecai ask Esther to do for the Jewish people?

SECOND DAY: Reread Esther 4:1-8 with the Scriptures listed in these questions.

1. Mordecai refused to put on the new clothes Esther offered him. He could have put on the new clothes, ignored the decree to kill the Jewish people of the kingdom, and gone on living just as he had been living. Of course, this would not change the facts and reality of the decree! There is another decree more sure and lasting that has been given to us by the King of kings. What is this decree found in Romans 3:22-25? Put these verses into your own words, if you wish.

82

2. What wonderful, good news do you find in Romans 6:22,23?

3. Isaiah 61:10 expresses the joy Christians feel when they have invited the Lord Jesus Christ into their life and experienced His forgiveness and love. Put this verse into your own words using your name in it, if you wish.

4. What color are the robes described in Revelation 7:9-17 and who are the people wearing them?

5 a. **Challenge:** White garments are spoken of a great deal in the Bible. What do the following verses say about them?

Matthew 17:1,2

Revelation 19:7,8

b. How is our own purity and righteousness described in Isaiah 64:6? How does this contrast to God's pure righteousness He longs to give us as we receive by faith His Son Jesus Christ?

6 (Personal) Have you ever tried to appear "religious" by taking on the customs and appearances of what you believe a Christian should be like? There are those who are able to deceive people this way, but there is one person we can never fool. Read 1 Samuel 16:7. What does it say?

THIRD DAY: Read Esther 4:9-17.

1. What reasonable arguments concerning her audience with the king and its potential dangers did Esther give to Mordecai?

2. What great challenge does Mordecai give Esther in Esther 4:14?

3 a. What was Esther's reply to Mordecai?

  b. Did Mordecai cooperate with Esther when asked?

  c. (Personal) When someone asks you to pray for them are you faithful to carry out the promise you gave to pray? Why not keep a prayer list or a notebook, and list those you are praying for, as well as answers to prayer by God?

4 a. (Personal) When you are asked to do something for the Lord in your church, community or fellowship, have you given God excuses and reasons why you can't serve Him? Have you given similar reasons to the people who ask you to serve the Lord? What blessings do you believe you have missed by saying no to a request after you have prayed about it and God seemed to be nudging you to say yes?

  b. Without mentioning a name, share how someone has been blessed by God through their obedience in service to Him. Can you think of an example of how a blessing was missed when someone bypassed an opportunity to serve the Lord in some way?

5. Christians have a motivator and an enabler, the Holy Spirit, who will give them the strength to meet God's opportunities for them, in His power and wisdom. Read John 16:7,13,14. What do you learn about the Holy Spirit in these verses?

6. **Challenge:** What do the following verses say concerning the Holy Spirit in the life of a Christian? Put these Scriptures into your own words, if you wish.

1 Corinthians 6:19,20

Ephesians 3:16; 6:17,18

FOURTH DAY: Read all of Esther 5 concentrating on verses 1-8.

1 a. What did Queen Esther do on the third day after fasting?

b. How did the king respond when he saw Esther?

2. What did the king say to Esther?

3. Think of how Esther must have felt as she stood in the doorway and caught the first glimpse of the king on his throne. As Christians there are many times when our emotions may be very similar to hers! How do the following promises from God's Word encourage you to step out in faith in new experiences and challenges with God? Personalize these verses with your own words.

Psalm 32:8

85

4. (Personal) What is your favorite verse in question 3? Did it give you some special encouragement to share with others?

5. Did Esther immediately tell the king what her request was? What did she ask him to do? (see Esther 5).

6 a. How does the last half of Isaiah 28:16 and Psalm 33:20 seem to reflect Esther's attitude in this crisis concerning the life or death of all the Jewish people in Ahasuerus's kingdom?

   b. (Personal) What about you? Who is the first one you turn to in a crisis for advice and help—God or man? Who do you think would give the best counsel?

   c. Note Esther 5:1 where Esther put on her finest royal dress before appearing before the king. How important do you think it is for a Christian to be properly dressed and well groomed? What are the dangers of thinking about our appearance too much, and what are the dangers in considering personal appearance too lightly?

FIFTH DAY: Read Esther 5:9-14.

1. Haman was pleased with the honor bestowed on him by the queen. Yet there was still a thorn in his flesh. What was it?

2. How does this reveal what Haman's personality was like? Describe what you believe his character traits were after reading Esther 5:9-14.

3 a. **Challenge:** How does the Bible warn us about personality traits similar to Haman's? Read the following verses.

Psalm 10:2-4

Proverbs 21:4

James 4:6

b. Can you think of any other verse you would like to share that deals with pride, envy, hatred or plotting? According to Proverbs 28:25, what must a person do to find God's leading, power, success and victory in life?

4 a. When Haman complained about Mordecai, what suggestion did his wife make in Esther 5:14?

b. How did Haman respond to this poor advice?

5. **Challenge:** Sometimes we are given good advice concerning a matter disturbing to us. As Christians we are to respond in a far different way than Haman did. How do you think the Christian should respond? Read some of these verses to help you think

through your answer: Proverbs 3:5,6; Psalm 23:2,3; 1 Thessalonians 5:21; 2 Timothy 1:7.

6. Review the verse in this lesson that you memorized this week. Write down the verse and its reference and keep it along with others you have learned. Keep them all in an accessible place so you can easily review your verses and grow spiritually.

SIXTH DAY: Read all the Notes and look up the Scriptures.

1. What new thought did you find helpful in the Notes?

2. What personal application did you select to apply to your own life this week?

Study Notes

When Haman is introduced in the book of Esther he had just been given the highest position the king of Persia could have given him, that similar to a prime minister. This high honor had gone to Haman's head, for he was very proud and vain. Therefore, when a porter at the gate did not bow to him as the king had commanded, Haman could not endure this indifference. In retaliation for this disobedience, Haman planned to kill all of the Jews in Persia. He presented his terrible plan to the king of Persia, which the king signed and sent to every province (see Esther 3).

It was decided that lots would be cast to determine the day when all of the Jewish people would be massacred. The lot fell on the thirteenth day of March, just 10 months away (see Esther 3:7). Haman wanted so much to make sure this edict be carried out that he offered to pay the king a $20 million bribe (see Esther 3:9). Imagine trying to bribe your king! And can you imagine the terror as the king's speediest couriers carried this dreaded written edict to the far corners of Persia. Jewish people in every village must have trembled as they heard what would happen in only 10 months. Imagine how you would feel if you knew you had only 10 month to live!

God Uses People to Perform His Miracles Esther 4:1-8

God could have chosen to deliver His doomed people, the Israelites, by means of a miracle. He had saved them many times before by miracles. But this time God chose to use people rather than a miraculous event to deliver His people from extinction.

Mordecai cried sadly and bitterly when he heard the predicament of his people, the Jews. Not only did he know what was publicly announced, he had a copy of the decree (see Esther 4:8). Mordecai was undoubtedly heavily grieved, for he realized it was his act of obedience and love to God by refusing to bow to Haman that brought Haman's wrath upon the Jewish people. Therefore, Mordecai put on sackcloth and ashes (see Esther 4:1), which was in those days a token of overwhelming grief (see Job 2:12; Dan. 9:3).

It is similar to the custom still practiced in some countries today, where a widow will wear black to show her grief at the loss of her husband. Because of Mordecai's "grieving clothes" he was not allowed within the king's gate. Why? It was probably because it was customary for kings in that day to refuse to have anyone in their court who was suffering sorrow or tragedy. Kings did not want to be touched by such emotions.

Nothing except happy and pleasant matters were brought to the king's court. Everything that was melancholy was forbidden. It was as if the king was attempting to forbid sickness, trouble or death to enter. The king of Persia did not know how to deal with such things, therefore, he tried to shut them out from his sight and hearing!

Our King Never Shuts Us Out!

We have a King who is always aware of our sickness, trouble and grief at the loss of a loved one. He does not try to shut Himself away from our troubles, but identifies with us in them and offers hidden sources of power through the Holy Spirit to take us through such crises. "In Him, you also, after listening to the message of truth, the gospel of your salvation—having also believed, you were sealed in Him with the Holy Spirit of promise" (Eph. 1:13, *NASB*).

The Holy Spirit gives us the inner power of God to meet such situations. Have you claimed forgiveness from God through the death of Christ on your behalf? Do you know that you have received the Holy Spirit, in whose Person the Lord Jesus has come to live within you? If you've not done this, why not make this decision now, and quietly bow your head and invite the Lord Jesus Christ into your life as Lord and Savior? "In whom we have redemption through his blood, the forgiveness of sins, according to the riches of his grace" (Eph. 1:7, *KJV*).

Now the Jews throughout all of Persia fasted and wept, and many of them, like Mordecai, wore sackcloth and ashes (see Esther 4:3). They denied themselves the comfort of food and soft clothing. Those who chose to stay and live comfortably in Persia, where they had been brought as captives, now must have wished that they too had returned to the land of Israel with the first group who had been released by an edict signed by King Cyrus (see Neh. 2).

> *The Holy Spirit gives us a conscience of conviction, which is absolutely from God and shows us right from wrong.*

Had they answered that first call from God to return to the land of Israel, they would not have been experiencing the sorrow of a death sentence. But it had been much more convenient for them to stay in the land of Persia, for many of them had become involved in the business and politics of the country and were successful citizens. It had seemed illogical to leave their comfort, to travel back to Israel and to struggle to rebuild a life there. Now they were suffering the consequences of what they had thought was doing right in making a moral choice.

A Conscience of Conviction

Today we frequently face making moral choices. The Holy Spirit gives us a conscience of conviction, which is absolutely from God and shows us right from wrong. Many Christians cannot explain this conscience except to say, "Deep down inside, I know what God wants me to say and do. At the same time I know God's warning signals that show me what I should not do and say!"

And so it is that Christians must either yield to the darkness of the tug of the flesh or to the light and beauty that comes from yielding to the leading of the Holy Spirit. When the Lord fills you, you know it. And the fruit of the Spirit will show itself in your life (see Gal. 5:22,23). When the Lord fills you, you will be full of joy and will find a peace beyond description.

God will also give you greater self-control to choose to follow the Holy Spirit's leading and thus to know His enabling power. Someone has said, "The Christian life without the fullness of the Holy Spirit is rather insipid or flat; it is like a soft drink without the fizz. Don't give up your search. I'm sorry it took me so long to be able to yield myself to Him." Romans 12:1,2 is a good place to start.

A Queen's Love for Her People

In Esther 4:5 we discover that Esther's maid and her chamberlains brought the news of Mordecai's sorrow to Esther. This grieved the queen greatly for his grief was hers. She respected and loved Mordecai very much. He had adopted her into his family and raised her as his own child when her parents died. Esther must have also thought of all of the other Jewish people's distress. Although she was a queen she never forgot her relationship to them.

Esther immediately sent clothing to Mordecai and hoped that he would remove his sackcloth in exchange for it. She undoubtedly recognized the law that said that no one could enter the royal gate in sackcloth. What her objective was in sending out new clothes the Bible does not disclose. It would seem that Esther probably wanted to hear the full story of the terrible edict, to kill all of the Jewish people, from Mordecai's own lips. This may have been her motive in these actions.

Others believe that some of the materialism of the king's court had rubbed off on Esther and she did not wish to have her foster father appearing in the city poorly dressed in sackcloth and ashes before the people. Later on as we read about her decision to lay her life on the line for the Jewish people, this seems an unlikely motive for Queen Esther. However, it does cause us to pause and reflect on our own motives as Christians concerning the life-style we choose in our culture today.

Who Are We Trying to Please?

What about the way we dress, the decoration of our homes, our choice of friends, the "front" we present to the world at large? Ask yourself these questions: Who am I trying to please or impress, man or God? Who am I trying to obey? Are you willing to say, "Whether it is good or evil, we will obey the voice of the Lord our God to whom we are sending you, that it may be well with us when we obey the voice of the Lord our God" (Jer. 42:6, *RSV*). The easiest way out is to plug our ears and not listen to the cry of the hungry, cold, war-torn world that's calling out for our love and God's love.

Though we face a different world today, with different tastes, interests and values, we must remember that the Lord Jesus Christ has not changed! (see Heb. 13:8). He loves us and wants to help us in our lives each day to be a blessing and a channel of His mercy and love to a strife-torn world. To minister to others in Christ's name may demand a change not only in our attitude of submissiveness to God's will, but also a change in our life-style. Are you willing to change if God asks you to?

Trust God to Care for His People

Esther sent Hatach, the man whom the king had appointed to attend her, to Mordecai outside the king's gate. She wanted a detailed account of the reason for Mordecai's mourning. In Esther 4:7 Mordecai told him "everything that had happened to him." He also sent her a copy of the king's edict so that she might see the eminent danger that she and her people were in! Mordecai stated to Hatach that if Esther had any respect for her uncle, or had any kindness for the Jewish nation, she would appear now before the king on their behalf. We do not know what action Mordecai expected the king to take, but obviously he was trusting God to care for the Jewish people.

Esther must have been particularly interested in the details concerning Haman's part in this planned slaughter of her race in Persia. Mordecai, by the providence of God, knew Esther needed to realize that Haman was a key man in these terrible plans. Indeed, he was already a key man in the kingdom, for the king had elevated him above all other court members! Thus Esther was warned by God through Mordecai of the kind of person she would be dealing with when she was in the presence of Haman. It was most important that Esther knew who her enemy was!

Knowledge of Our Enemy Is Important

It is important for Christians today to know who the enemy is in order that we might resist him by the power of God (see Eph. 4:27; 6:11-16; Jas. 4:7). The Lord Jesus Christ offers victory over Satan (see Heb. 2:14) and we know that Satan will ultimately be destroyed forever (see Rev. 20:10).

We must look outside ourselves for the answer to our problems with Satan. Can we be victorious over this enemy who tempts, accuses, distracts and destroys? The answer is yes! There is day-to-day victory available to every Christian in conflict, and it is possible to stand firm and see the defeat of every trick of Satan. God has "delivered us from the power of darkness, and hath translated us into the kingdom of his dear Son" (Col. 1:13, KJV). Yes, He has done this for us. At the heart of the victory over Satan is the finished work of the Lord Jesus Christ upon the cross. He who died for our sins according to the Scriptures, who was buried, and who rose again from the dead, gives us the victory! (see 1 John 5:18; Rom. 16:20).

We Need Knowledge of God's Word

It is essential that we have a knowledge of the Bible as we "stand against the wiles of the devil" (Eph. 6:11, KJV). The Lord Jesus Christ used three thrusts of the sword, the Word of God, when He was tempted by Satan in the wilderness (see Matt. 4:1-11). Nothing can explain the weakness of a Christian more clearly than the ignorance of the Word of God. This condition cannot be cured by reading a verse a day or by reading a book about the Bible.

In order to use the Scriptures in our daily living and victoriously in our lives, we need to take time to read and reread God's inspired words, the Bible. It's true that by this method God's ways will become our ways, because He will have spoken to us through His Word. "How sweet are thy words to my taste! Yea, sweeter than honey to my mouth! Through thy precepts I get understanding: therefore I hate every false way. Thy word is a lamp unto my feet, and a light unto my path" (Ps. 119:103-105, KJV).

Knowledge of Prayer Is Essential

In our weapons against Satan, there is also prayer. As we think of Esther going before the king on behalf of her people and herself, we can see a parallel of the Christian approaching God in prayer through the Lord Jesus Christ on behalf of himself and others. "Satan trembles when he sees the weakest saint upon his knees" (William Cowper).

God does fortify us against Satan and gives us strength, comfort and guidance in each temptation, just as He did for the Lord Jesus Christ when He was tempted three times by Satan. "Yours is the mighty power and glory and victory and majesty. Everything in the heavens and earth is yours, O Lord, and this is your kingdom. We adore you as being in control of everything" (1 Chron. 29:11, *TLB*). Prayer is an essential communication between God and ourselves. It plays a part in victory over Satan. Are you spending time each day in prayer with the Lord?

Courage in the Face of Fear Esther 4:9-17

Hatach, one of the king's chamberlains, brought all the details concerning the edict to Esther. Again Esther sent a message back to Mordecai by way of this man. She stated that she could not go to the king without peril to her life, and she had not been called before the king for 30 days. There was a death sentence for anyone who entered the court without invitation. The only exception was when the king would hold out his golden sceptre and invite someone to come forward even though uninvited (see Esther 4:11). Esther probably felt that since she had not been called into the king's presence for 30 days, she had little chance of being accepted into the court.

This law made the royal palace little more than a royal prison! As we ponder on the foolishness of such a law and the terror of those who had to obey it, we realize there are people in our society today living under almost the same circumstances! Many individuals have made their lives miserable by their own haughtiness and bad temper. Certainly this should not be true of the Christian who is yielding to the Holy Spirit (see Gal. 5:22,23). Let us always be sure to be hospitable, humble, showing forth the love of Christ to those who knock upon our door with their needs.

One example of hospitality is to invite foreign students into your home. It's one of the ways to take "a trip around the world" without leaving your living room! Before you open your home, it would be wise to brief your family, from your encyclopedia, about the country from which your guest comes. Of course you will learn much more by asking your guest questions and looking at pictures he or she may

94

have. This activity benefits all participants; it's a good lesson in social studies if there are children in the home and a refresher course for adults. Not only can you be a goodwill ambassador for your country, but foremost you are being a goodwill ambassador for the Lord Jesus Christ (see 2 Cor. 5:20). There is real joy in serving the Lord by sharing His love with others.

Poised in God's Promises

Mordecai's faith in God and God's providence for the Jewish people is found in Esther 4:14: "For if you remain silent at this time, relief and deliverance will arise for the Jews from another place and you and your father's house will perish" (*NASB*). Mordecai knew the promises of God and the history of Israel. He had no doubt that God would rescue the Jewish people out of this situation just as He had done so many times before. This passage is a key to the basic meaning of the entire book of Esther. It demonstrates the unfailing providence of God in behalf of His people, Israel.

Esther responded to Mordecai's message by asking him to fast and pray with her for three days before she went before the king. She promised that both she and her maidens would fast. Possibly the maidens were Jewish women or proselytes to the faith whom Esther had taught to pray. Prayer to God is not mentioned here, but it is quite obviously implied (see Joel 1:14). After three days and nights, Esther sent her reply to Mordecai, "If I perish, I perish" (Esther 4:16, *KJV*). She was willing to die for her people and her Lord. Willingness to die is the price that all Christians must be willing to pay if we want to be raised from the dead to live, work and walk in the power of the Holy Spirit (see Rom. 12:1,2; Col. 3:1-4).

When we think of three days and three nights, we find some very significant events in the Bible before and after Esther's time. For example, it was on the third morning that Joshua took the Israelites into the depths of the Jordan. They were preserved miraculously by God's intervention (see Deut. 31:7,8; Joshua 3, 4). "That all the people of the earth might know the hand of the Lord, that it is mighty: that ye might fear the Lord your God for ever" (Josh. 4:24, *KJV*).

Even before the account of Joshua, there was a third morning when "Abraham lifted up his eyes, and saw the place afar off" (Gen. 22:4, *KJV*). God had asked Abraham to take his son Isaac to offer him as a sacrifice to God. Then God provided a ram in the thicket as a substitute for Isaac, who was the only son to carry on the line for the family of Israel. God worked this miracle not only to increase Abraham's faith and obedience to Him, but to give us an example to take up that challenge to trust and obey.

In another course, we will study the book of Jonah, who was in the belly of the whale three days and three nights. God worked another miracle and not only preserved Jonah physically, but changed his attitudes and actions, as well.

> *There are many times in the life of a Christian when God's plan hangs in a delicate balance. It is when we are called to that challenge, when we are obedient, that Christ who is waiting to empower us does so!*

And, of course, there is that mighty power of the third morning when the Lord Jesus Christ was resurrected. Here again God used a time period of three days and three nights.

God Will Provide Us with a Plan Esther 5:1-8

Imagine Esther, rather weakened after three days of fasting, crossing through the royal palace to the royal court to present herself uninvited to the king! What an amazing example of obedience to God we find here! For our benefit God has preserved the story to show not only His providence, but also to show a human being's faithfulness and obedience to God. There are many times in the life of a Christian when God's plan hangs in a delicate balance. It is when we are called to that challenge, when we are obedient, that Christ who is waiting to empower us does so! Can you sense Esther's combination of fright and excitement as you consider what God might challenge you to do in the near future?

Again we see God's providence as Queen Esther found favor in his sight (see Esther 5:2) and was allowed to enter the court. Can't you just imagine Esther's sigh of relief as she walked forward to touch the top of the king's golden sceptre?

There may come a time when you will be constrained to do something very difficult as the Holy Spirit nudges at the very center of your being. Any of you who have been obedient to the Holy Spirit's touch knows, as you begin by taking that first step, you do not walk alone, but God walks with you all the way. It is amazing that when we obey God at such times, He works wonderful miracles in the lives of people who need His help and love. When it is God's time and His providence, are you willing to be His person "for such a time as this?" (Esther 4:14).

Apparently during these three days and three nights in which Esther fasted, God had given her a plan. He had directed her to give some dinner parties! Surely she must have trusted God to have contained herself from rushing forward with tears, explaining to the king the plight of her people in the land of Persia! Undoubtedly the king could tell from Esther's face that she had not stopped by for a small matter.

It was for this reason that he must have immediately asked Esther, "What can I do for you?" (see Esther 5:3). The king offered to give Esther half of his kingdom. He could sense that she had a great need. The chapter closes with Esther inviting Haman and the king to a banquet in her home. They attended, and the king again asked what her desire was. Esther told him that she would respond with her need the next night when Haman and the king again came to her home to dine (see Esther 5:6-8).

Not All Plans Come from God Esther 5:9-14

Can you imagine how joyful Haman was to be invited for dinner to the queen's quarters with only the king? But on the way home he saw Mordecai at the king's gate and again Mordecai refused to bow down to him. This made Haman furious; he must have raced home to share both his joy, and frustration, with his family.

The Scripture says in Esther 5:10 that he called not only his wife, but also his friends to his side so that he could share with them the excitement of the day. Boastfully he told of the wealth he possessed, and the multitude of his children. He also bragged about his important position as the highest man in the land next to the king. Then he told about his dinner invitation with the king to Queen Esther's quarters the next evening.

After sharing all these things, Haman vented his frustrations by telling them about Mordecai and all that had happened at the king's gate that day (see Esther 5:13). His pagan wife Zeresh and his friends gave some very poor advice, which pleased Haman! They advised him to hang Mordecai the next day. Haman immediately ordered the gallows to be made (see Esther 5:14). They were to be constructed 75 feet high to guarantee that everyone would see the downfall of Mordecai. In this passage, we see the contrast between a real woman of God, Esther, who was willing to give her life for her people and completely trusted God in the situation, and Zeresh, a pagan woman making her own evil plans to further her husband, Haman.

OUR PERFECT STRENGTH AND SHIELD

ESTHER 6 AND 7

Before you begin your study this week:
1. Pray and ask God to speak to you through His Holy Spirit each day.
2. Use only your Bible for your answers.
3. Write down your answers and the verses you have used.
4. Challenge questions are for those who have the time and wish to do them.
5. Personal questions are to be shared with your study group only if you wish to share.
6. As you study look for a verse to memorize this week. Write it down, carry it with you, tack it to your bulletin board, tape it to the dashboard of your car. Make a real effort to learn the verse and its reference.

FIRST DAY: Read Esther 6 concentrating on verses 1-3.

1. Who was unable to sleep and what did he do about his insomnia?

2. How did the king's insomnia become a factor in the deliverance of the Jewish people from the death penalties he had agreed to earlier? (see Esther 3:8-10, Esther 2:21-23 and Esther 6:2,3).

3 a. **Challenge:** Have you ever tried to help someone who is in need, or tried to serve the Lord according to His plan in other ways, and then found yourself in distressing circumstances? Have you wondered what kind of a reward this was? God has given us the answer to these questions not only through Mordecai's experiences but also through many other Scriptures. How do the following verses help you to understand difficult experiences that occur in spite of your obedience to God's plans? Personalize these verses by adding your own name.

Isaiah 54:17

Matthew 10:29-32 (Note: These are the Lord Jesus' words to Christians.)

Galatians 6:9

b. (Personal) Reread the verses in Esther 6:3. Which helped you the most?

4. Since sleeplessness was a key factor in working out God's plan for Mordecai, do you have any changed attitudes about insomnia?

5. (Personal) Do you identify with the problem of occasional sleeplessness or perhaps with frequent insomnia? Has this passage in Esther been helpful to you in any way concerning your attitudes about sleep?

6. What other helpful promises does God offer you concerning sleep as you rest by faith in Him? (See Psalm 4:8 and Proverbs 3:24, or use another passage of Scripture you have found.)

SECOND DAY: Read Esther 6:4-12.

1 a. Who was in the king's outer court during the time the king could not sleep?

   b. Why had this person come to the court?

   c. What question did the king ask this man? Give verse.

2. Since Haman thought he was the one to be honored, what plan did he dream up?

3. What order did the king give to Haman in Esther 6:10 that must have shocked him and hurt his pride?

4 a. Haman had to obey his king's orders and did just that. What did he do after honoring Mordecai?

   b. Where did Mordecai go after he was honored? Does this indicate any particular character traits he might have had?

5. As you consider the king's remembrance of how Mordecai saved his life what good characteristics do you find the king had? (see Esther 2:21-23 with Esther 6).

6. (Personal) Have you ever stopped what you were doing when you were reminded that you needed to show gratitude, to help someone who in need, or right a bruised or broken relationship? Share,

if possible, your experience of God's blessing when you have responded to His nudging in some way.

THIRD DAY: Read Esther 6:13,14 with Esther 7:1-4.

1 a. When Haman returned to his home who was there? What did he tell these people?

   b. What did these people tell Haman?

   c. While Haman was talking in his home about the honors Mordecai had received, who came to his home and what did they want?

2 a. How does Genesis 12:3, which speaks of the Jewish people, foretell Haman's fate?

   b. **Challenge:** What promise of the Savior Jesus Christ do you find in Genesis 12:3?

3. **Challenge:** Generations later the promise of God in Genesis 12:3 was kept when the Lord Jesus Christ left His heavenly home to come to earth as perfect God-perfect Man. How do the following verses express why He came to earth?

Luke 19:10

John 1:29

Matthew 1:21

4 a. How do the following verses help you to understand Jesus Christ and the need to receive Him into your life?

John 14:6

Acts 4:12

  b. (Personal) Have you ever come by way of Jesus Christ into the family of God?

5. In Esther 7:1-4, what does the king ask Esther?

6. From that same passage, what request does Esther make to the king?

FOURTH DAY: Read Esther 7:5-10.

1 a. What second question did the king ask Esther and how did she dare to answer it?

  b. Haman's sins of hatred and vengeance had been revealed. How did he feel according to Esther 7:6?

2 a. Where did the king go to think more clearly about Esther's request and accusation and how he should respond to it?

b. How were Haman's emotions demonstrated by his actions? See Esther 7:7,8.

3.a. When the king came in and saw Haman's actions, what did the king apparently order the servants or guards to do?

b. What was the fate of wicked Haman?

4 a. **Challenge:** Read Galatians 6:7-9. What part of this passage could describe Haman's life?

b. (Personal) Reread Galatians 6:7-9. How would you like this passage to relate to your life?

5. Haman was hung on a gallows and died as a result of his personal sins. Who was hung on a cross to die for our personal sins? Use key thoughts from the two verses below.

Philippians 2:8-11

Hebrews 12:2

6 a. **Challenge:** Who undoubtedly suffered as a result of Haman's sins?

b. (Personal) Can you think of instances today where others have suffered as a result of someone else's sin? How does this serve as a personal warning to you to seek God's forgiveness and deliverance from sin?

FIFTH DAY: Read Psalm 108 with Esther 6 and 7 in mind.

1. Which verses do you feel could be an expression of Esther's cry for help for herself and her people before she saw God's deliverance?

2. Which verses do you believe could express Esther and Mordecai's emotions of thankfulness to God for His deliverance? Write the central thought of each verse you list.

3. (Personal) Which of the verses in this Psalm do you wish to choose as your prayer of praise or request to God today?

4. Review the verse in this lesson that you memorized this week. Write down the verse and its reference and keep it, along with others you have learned, in an accessible place. Then you can easily review your verses and grow spiritually.

SIXTH DAY: Read all the Notes and look up the Scriptures.

1. What new thought did you find helpful in the Notes?

2. What personal application did you select to apply to your own life this week?

Study Notes

"That night the king could not sleep" (Esther 6:1). Sleep, which is a gift from God, was withheld from King Ahasuerus. The king, who commanded 127 provinces, could not command one hour's sleep! The thoughts being tossed about in his mind, which resulted in sleeplessness, are not divulged by the Scriptures.

Perhaps the king was troubled with guilt, because he had been made aware that he had neglected his beloved queen for 30 days (see Esther 4:11). Guilt feelings can certainly contribute to insomnia, but there could have been other reasons why the king lost sleep. One reason might have been his curiosity concerning the queen's request, which she had refused to divulge that night at the banquet in her quarters (see Esther 5:6-8).

The queen had promised the king that if he would return for dinner the following evening she would tell him her request. Maybe the king was contemplating the countless requests that Esther might ask of him, which in turn started a merry-go-round of thoughts that would not turn off, resulting in insomnia!

Could There Be a Reason for No Sleep?

Though the king was unaware of it, God had a purpose for his sleepless night. Now the king could have called the court physician to prescribe some medication for his insomnia. He could have had a warm glass of milk and some of his favorite food brought to him to help lull him to sleep. Or he could have called for the court musicians, just as a person today can flip a switch to turn on soft music to help him get to sleep. But God had a different plan for this particular sleepless night! God wanted him to read the book of the chronicles. He would use it to remind the king of Mordecai's kindness to him some years previous.

The king commanded that the book of the chronicles be brought in and read to him. It would be much like reading a child to sleep. However, this particular night the selected portion of the book of the chronicles revealed something so exciting and surprising that the king probably didn't get any sleep at all! "And it was found written, that Mordecai had told of Bigthana and Teresh, two of the king's chamberlains, the keepers of the door, who sought to lay hand on the king Ahasuerus" (Esther 6:2, *KJV*).

The king immediately took interest in an event in his life he had forgotten. He wanted to know if the man who saved his life, Mordecai, had ever been rewarded. The king's servants replied, "There is nothing done for him" (Esther 6:3, *KJV*). We see some good characteristics in the king at this point as he remembered to be grateful, even though he had been forgetful for some time. When he was reminded of Mordecai's help, he set about immediately to seek the best way to honor this man.

Is There Something You Need to Do?

Have you ever been reminded of something and stopped what you were doing to show gratitude to someone? What do you do when you see someone in need? When you sense a broken or bruised relationship, do you hasten to do all you can to restore that relationship with another person? God will bless those who humble themselves and respond to His nudging. "The reward for humility and fear of the Lord is riches and honor and life" (Prov. 22:4, *RSV*). "Honor shall uphold the humble in spirit" (Prov. 29:23, *KJV*). The Bible scholar Matthew Henry said, "Though the aspiring rise fast, the humble stand fast."

You Reap What You Sow

Keep in mind that whatever a man sows, he will reap. If you sow potatoes, you'll get potatoes. If you sow corn, you'll get corn. "Do not be deceived: God cannot be mocked. A man reaps what he sows. The one who sows to please his sinful nature, from that nature will reap destruction; the one who sows to please the Spirit, from the Spirit will reap eternal life" (Gal. 6:7,8).

We will see Haman experience the harvest of corruption, which he had sown by the decree he had drawn up against the Jews, in order to rid himself of his enemy Mordecai. Throughout the pages of history, there have been many other men who have reaped a similar harvest, men such as Hitler and Mussolini. Truly the Word of God promises great blessings for those who humbly seek the Lord and follow after Him, but also warns that the wicked will suffer for their actions. "I have seen the wicked in great power, and spreading himself like a green bay tree. Yet he passed away, and, lo, he was not: yea, I sought him, but he could not be found" (Ps. 37:35,36, *KJV*).

If we make a daily, moment by moment practice of "sowing," or "yielding" our lives to the Holy Spirit, we will find that the Lord can make beautiful harmony from our lives. A harmony that cannot be exhibited unless we are willing to listen to the Holy Spirit and to obey when God nudges us to action.

Man Proposes . . . God Disposes Esther 6:4-14

It seems that Haman's carpenters worked most of the night to build the gallows (see Esther 5:14), and then Haman went to the king's court early in the morning to ask the king's permission to have Mordecai hanged. Before he had a chance to ask his important question, the king said, "Who is in the court?" (Esther 6:4, *KJV*). He had Haman called to his side in the throne room to answer a question. Haman had wanted to get to the court before any business had been brought before the king. He wanted to ask for a warrant to hang Mordecai immediately. Haman had not counted on this twist of events!

Apparently the king wanted to ask his statesman about honoring Mordecai and Haman happened to be the only statesman in the court at such an early hour. One rule of the kingdom was that a king must never be obligated to a captive and this may have played a part in the king's energies to reward Mordecai immediately. The amazing thing here is God's providence! Just as the king was preparing to honor Mordecai, Haman came in for permission to hang him! There is an old saying that is illustrated here: "Man proposes . . . God disposes."

We Can Rest in Faith

Do you identify with the problem of occasional sleeplessness or perhaps with frequent insomnia? Certainly this passage in Esther is helpful, then, as we see that God can work in such a problem. Hopefully, fear is not at the root of insomnia for a Christian.

> *God expects us to use the insight He has given us to obtain a proper balance in our lives as far as sleep and work are concerned.*

God has given us many helpful promises concerning sleep as you rest in faith in the Lord Jesus Christ. "I will lie down in peace and sleep, for though I am alone, O Lord, you will keep me safe" (Ps. 4:8, *TLB*; see also Prov. 3:24.) Yet, God warns that we should not place too much emphasis on sleep. In fact, the Christian is cautioned about sleep in this way in Proverbs 20:13: "If you love sleep, you will end in poverty. Stay awake, work hard, and there will be plenty to eat!" (*TLB*). Thus we see that God expects us to use the insight He has given us to obtain a proper balance in our lives as far as sleep and work are concerned.

At a medical congress not long ago, a well-known nerve specialist made this statement: "As one whose whole life has been concerned with the sufferings of the mind, I would state that of all the hygienic measures to counteract disturbed sleep, depression of spirit, and all the miserable sequels of a distressed mind, I would undoubtedly give the first place to the simple habit of prayer" (*The Friend*).

A Case of the Wrong Man

Now the king was fully persuaded that Haman was a man of integrity and would be able to help him honor Mordecai. Thus as Haman walked into the court he was greeted by the king with this question, "What is to be done for the man whom the king desires to honor?" (Esther 6:6, *NASB*). We see Haman's inflated ego as he said to himself, "Whom would the king desire to honor more than me?" (Esther 6:6, *NASB*). Therefore Haman thought quickly and suggested plans that were designed to please and honor himself. He gave specific details: the way he would like to be dressed, then mounted on the king's own horse, and given a parade down the main thoroughfare of the city. Heralds would lead him on horseback proclaiming all his great deeds to the people! (see Esther 6:7-9). After all, wouldn't this be an appropriate honor for the king's favorite and the one who was invited to dine exclusively with the king and queen two nights in a row?

Haman naturally assumed that his request to put Mordecai on the gallows in the garden of his home was quite obviously going to be granted, since he was such a favorite in the court. What he did not realize was that in the providence of God, Mordecai was going to be honored. Haman had planned and plotted against Mordecai, but if God did not want his child touched, Haman could go only so far with these plans. So it is with Satan today, as he plans and plots against the Christian; we can be sure that God is in control, has a plan for our lives, and is much more powerful than Satan. "Ye are of God, little children, and have overcome them: because greater is he that is in you than he that is in the world" (1 John 4:4, *KJV*).

Just imagine the shock it was to Haman when the king said, "Take quickly the robes and the horse as you have said, and do so for Mordecai the Jew, who is sitting at the king's gate; do not fall short in anything of all that you have said" (Esther 6:10, *NASB*). He must have been horrified to have discovered that it was Mordecai who was to have been honored rather than himself! Yet he was clever enough to hide his emotion.

Haman had to obey the king's orders, and went out from the court to honor Mordecai in exactly the way we had hoped to be honored (see Esther 6:11). Thus rather than hanging the man he hated so much, Haman had to carry out the plans for the grand parade to honor his sworn enemy. The clothing was brought and Mordecai was dressed up, then rode through the city. He was recognized as the king's favorite that day.

It would be difficult to determine if the task were more difficult for Haman, as he had to give honor to Mordecai, or for humble Mordecai to accept this honor from the king by the hand of Haman! Apparently such an honor was acceptable to Mordecai for it was an indication of the king's favor, and gave him hope that Esther would be able to influence the king to reverse the edict against the Jews.

Honored, Yet Humble

After the parade Mordecai returned to the king's gate. He had always been at the king's gate (see Esther 2:21; 3:3; 4:2) and was faithful to this responsibility of being accessible to Esther, his adopted daughter, while she lived in the court. The question we need to ask ourselves is how accessible are we to people who may need us? Are we willing to let God make us accessible and humble in this way?

The following story illustrates how two Christians were willing to humble themselves and go to faraway lands as God's instruments to bring Jesus Christ's Good News to others. "Ao's grandfather was a headhunter, as all the tribesmen in Nagaland were. Village fought against village. Hatred, animosity and bloodshed had been their way of life since they could remember.

God may never call you to a faraway land, but He is calling you to be responsive when there is someone with a need!

"Then one day a missionary came and told them of Jesus and His love. One by one, the Ao Nagas began to open their hearts to the message of salvation. Over a period of time, the killings stopped, whole villages accepted Christ and love for others replaced hatred. The church became the center of village activities. In Ao's village two thousand people meet each Lord's Day to worship God. And from this church Ao was sent to Bible school to prepare to lead his people.

"Ao came to America to learn more about Sunday school work. Leaving his wife and four little children at home, he waited weeks in Calcutta before his visa was granted. Now he is studying in America. How his face shone as he showed me pictures of his family. Church

110

leaders ask Ao to direct Sunday school work in their tribes and to train the Sunday school teachers. What a great opportunity to prepare the church of tomorrow" (Glint Newsletter).

Christians Are God's Hands and Feet

God may never call you to a faraway land, but He is calling you to be responsive when there is someone with a need! You are His hands, His feet, His voice if you are a Christian. The question is, Are you willing to be the humble servant? "And so, dear brothers, I plead with you to give your bodies to God. Let them be a living sacrifice, holy—the kind he can accept. When you think of what he has done for you, is this too much to ask? Don't copy the behavior and customs of this world, but be a new and different person with a fresh newness in all you do and think. Then you will learn from your own experience how his ways will really satisfy you" (Rom. 12:1,2, *TLB*).

Some Schemes Lead to Humiliation

Haman hurried to his home and was in mourning. He had his head covered according to the custom of that day. He was utterly humiliated and told his wife and all his friends about the events that had just occurred (see Esther 6:13). Apparently these friends had remained with his wife while he went to the king's court to ask permission to hang Mordecai on the 75-foot-high gallows (see Esther 5:14). They had not wanted to miss the great event, but in remaining in Haman's house they had missed the honoring of Mordecai! Zeresh, Haman's wife and all of his friends told him, "If Mordecai is a Jew, you will never succeed in your plans against him; to continue to oppose him will be fatal" (Esther 6:13, *TLB*).

One Woman's Total Commitment Esther 7:1-4

While Haman was discussing these matters with friends, the king's messengers arrived to take him to Esther's banquet. The king was to be there also. Haman did not realize the fate that awaited him. "Pride goeth before destruction, and an haughty spirit before a fall" (Prov.16:18, *KJV*). We will see this illustrated in the life of Haman in Esther 7.

During the second banquet Esther had prepared for the king and Haman, the king again requested that Esther share her petition with him. Again he offered to give her "even half of the kingdom" if she desired it (see Esther 7:2). Actually this was the third time the king had asked for Esther's request (see Esther 5:3; 5:6; 7:2).

Imagine Esther's hesitancy and fear as she states her request at long last. "If I have found favor in your sight, O king, and if it please the king, let my life be given me as my petition, and my people as my request; for we have been sold, I and my people, to be destroyed, to be killed and to be annihilated. Now if we had only been sold as slaves, men and women, I would have remained silent, for the trouble would not be commensurate with the annoyance to the king" (Esther 7:3,4, *NASB*).

This must have been a tremendous moment for Esther as she now gave herself in total commitment to her people by making this request. Indeed she identified herself as a Jewess! This was an unknown fact since Mordecai, her adoptive father, had entered her in the beauty contest and instructed her not to tell her nationality to anyone (see Esther 2:20).

Cast Down, but Not Destroyed

Esther's courage reminds us of the courage of Christians who are persecuted for their faith in Jesus Christ, yet will not deny their faith in Him as their Savior and their Lord. "We are troubled on every side, yet not distressed; we are perplexed, but not in despair; persecuted, but not forsaken; cast down, but not destroyed" (2 Cor. 4:8,9, *KJV*).

You may ask yourself, Is there a persecution of Christians today under East European Communist regimes? Marxist-Leninist exponents are offended at the question. They point out that churches are still open and that only "enemies of peace and detente" would make such "unfactual" statements. An objective picture of the actual conditions in Czechoslovakia has just become available through the arrival in the West of a secret program for the annihilation of Christianity. It concerns Orava, the most northern part of Slovakia, little visited by tourists, but a land of beautiful scenery and rich cultural tradition (E.P. News Service).

Another example of present-day persecution is an open letter written to Christians all over the world from Russians concerning the treatment of Christian believers in the Soviet Union. "All of us, wives of the servants of the Lord, for a long time have become accustomed to constant searches, uninterrupted surveillance, thousands of anonymous letters filled with slander and the arrests of our husbands.

"We have become accustomed to standing at prison walls or at the barbed wire enclosures of prison camps for the purpose of passing on to our husbands the rare help permitted, or to wait until we would be allowed to interview them. I already have become accustomed to considering myself alone for the sake of the Lord, because since 1961—I have reared our nine children alone, leaning on the Lord. During the first five of these thirteen years my husband came home secretly on three occasions for periods of two to three days.

"Then followed prison and work camps for three years. During the last four years the children have not seen their father once, and I, because of continued surveillance, at great risk am meeting him less frequently than would be possible if he were in a prison camp. But God is remarkably granting us grace to bear these trials with joy and thanksgiving to Him" (*Gospel Call*, November 1974).

A Tyrant Is Unmasked! Esther 7:5-10

Esther had presented her petition, not for wealth or honor, not for the appointment of a friend to some high post, but for the preservation from death of herself and her people. This request so startled the king that he immediately asked, "Who is he, and where is he, who would presume to do thus?" (Esther 7:5, *NASB*).

The king wanted to know who could contrive such a murder plan. Esther, pointing her finger at Haman, responded, "A foe and an enemy, is this wicked Haman!" (Esther 7:6, *NASB*). This accusation, though it was true, absolutely terrified Haman. The queen was his prosecutor; the king was to be his judge; and his own conscience certainly must have been a witness against him. Picture him reclining upon the couch one moment, like a prime minister, having full confidence in his influence over the king, and suddenly having the props utterly knocked from beneath him. The tyrant had been unmasked before the king.

The king rose from the table in great anger and went into the palace garden to cool himself off and to consider what was to be done (see Esther 7:7). He had seven wise counselors according to historical writings, whom he could have called in to consult about the situation. However, he went to walk alone in the garden, determined to make his own decision concerning this matter. The king must have thought of what a fool he had been, to have been talked into making an edict that would doom not only his beloved queen, but a guiltless people to destruction (see Esther 3:8-11).

Could this be a warning to Christians today to never make a decision without first taking it to the Lord Jesus Christ and presenting it before Him for His wisdom and direction? If you make a practice of doing this, you will not have to be rushing out into your "palace garden" to ponder the results of a wrong decision, which may not only hurt you but many others, as well. "Pray without ceasing; in everything give thanks; for this is God's will for you in Christ Jesus. Do not quench the Spirit . . . Now may the God of peace Himself sanctify you entirely; and may your spirit and soul and body be preserved complete, without blame at the coming of our Lord Jesus Christ" (1 Thess. 5:17-19,23, *NASB*).

When the king re-entered the room, he was even more exasperated with Haman as he saw him laying, begging for his life at Esther's feet (see Esther 7:8). Self-willed, arrogant Haman had turned into a frightened coward. This man was so distraught that he threw himself to the floor beside the queen's couch and begged for his life.

Judgment Follows Evil

Haman who had mercilessly given the Jews no chance for a hearing now was confronted by the same kind of justice. The king was in a rage when he saw the scene before him. And he didn't take time for a trial! He needed to hear no more. Here was the man before him who had plotted to take the life of Mordecai, the one whom he had honored for saving the king's life. They covered Haman's head with the death hood, according to custom. The case against Haman was very clear. There was no need for a judge or jury.

And so one of the king's chamberlains suggested, "'Behold indeed, the gallows standing at Haman's house fifty cubits high, which Haman made for Mordecai who spoke good on behalf of the king!' And the king said, 'Hang him on it.' So they hanged Haman on the gallows which he had prepared for Mordecai, and the king's anger subsided" (Esther 7:9,10, *NASB*). Speedy judgment had come to Haman.

God Will Hear Your Pleadings

Are you in a situation that could be compared to Esther's? Then your prayer might be similar to the one found in Psalm 28. "Oh, praise the Lord, for he has listened to my pleadings! He is my strength, my shield from every danger. I trusted in him, and he helped me. Joy rises in my heart until I burst out in songs of praise to him. The Lord protects his people and gives victory to his anointed king" (vv. 6-8, *TLB*).

> USE ME DEAR LORD AS YOU SEE FIT.
> I would not change Your perfect will one bit.
> Mold me Lord and use me, beginning today
> Keeping me close to You, never to stray.
> Until that fine day, in heaven above
> I may dwell in Your presence surrounded by love.
> And see the face of my Savior dear
> Kneeling, His hands wipe away every tear.
> —Donna Pace

A MARVELOUS DELIVERANCE

ESTHER 8, 9 AND 10

Before you begin your study this week:
1. Pray and ask God to speak to you through His Holy Spirit each day.
2. Use only your Bible for your answers.
3. Write down your answers and the verses you have used.
4. Challenge questions are for those who have the time and wish to do them.
5. Personal questions are to be shared with your study group only if you wish to share.
6. As you study look for a verse to memorize this week. Write it down, carry it with you, tack it to your bulletin board, tape it to the dashboard of your car. Make a real effort to learn the verse and its reference.

FIRST DAY: Read Esther 8 concentrating on verses 1-5. Also review Esther 6 and 7.

1 a. What did the king give to Queen Esther that had belonged to Haman?

b. What secret relationship did Esther now reveal to King Ahasuerus? (see Esther 2:7,10 with Esther 8:1).

c. What honor did the king and Esther give to her cousin Mordecai?

2. Mordecai had been hated by Haman and Haman had planned to persecute him (see Esther 3). Haman hated all the Jews because of Mordecai and chose to persecute all the Jews because of that. God speaks to us in the Bible concerning the persecution of Christians by unbelievers. Put the following verses into your own words and personalize them, or simply write them as you find them. They all speak of this kind of persecution.

   1 Peter 3:13-15,17

   1 Peter 4:12-14

   2 Timothy 2:12,13

3. Which of these verses helped you the most?

4. **Challenge:** Read Psalm 73:3-20 and think of Haman who plotted to kill the Jews and seemed to flourish for a time (see Esther 3-8). How does this Psalm seem to describe God's final judgment on wicked Haman?

5. Apply Psalm 73:3-20 to some present-day situation in which you do not understand why the wicked seem to be flourishing.

SECOND DAY: Read Esther 8:6-10.

1. As you read Esther 8:6, think of the Lord Jesus who promised to suddenly return. Think of your friends, neighbors, business associates and family who are not ready to meet Christ because they have never come in simple faith to Him as Lord and Savior. Read Luke 9:26 with Esther 8:6. What does each verse say? How do these two verses challenge you as a Christian?

2. **Challenge:** Read Matthew 25:31-46 with Ephesians 6:6,7, Acts 17:31, Romans 2:16 and John 14:6,19. Does this help you to understand why the Lord Jesus Christ will be the final judge of mankind? Explain.

3. (Personal) What decisive action do you feel God would enable you to take this week, by the power of the Holy Spirit, in order to help some person know and receive the Lord Jesus Christ as personal Savior and Lord? List specific means by which you could take advantage of opportunities.

4. Because Esther dared to ask the king for something that would violate the king's law, he responded with a new law (see Esther 8:8-10). This new law delivered the Jewish people from the slaughter Haman had planned and negotiated for (see Esther 3:8-15). Esther pleaded with the king when it seemed hopeless! What about you? Are you guilty of feeling that certain social ills are impossible to change and correct? Do you just throw up your hands and say, "It's impossible to change this. Isn't it a sad situation?" Think of society today. Is there some problem that has concerned you? Do you believe God could use you to bring about a solution?

117

5. (Personal) Be specific! What problem or problems in your society has God called to your attention? What do you believe are the steps God would have you take to correct these wrongs?

THIRD DAY: Read Esther 8:9-17.

1. Note how the survival of the Jewish race depended on Esther and Mordecai's faithfulness in writing a letter! Do you believe God uses His people today to write letters or telephone to get out the message of His love and concern for all people?

2. (Personal) How about you? How responsive are you when God nudges you to write a letter or telephone someone?

3 a. Who actually wrote the letters in different languages for each province as Mordecai and Esther directed them?

   b. Can you think of people who fulfill similar functions today?

   c. (Personal) Do you believe God might call you to be a letter writer to some needy person today?

4. How does Esther 8:16 describe the Jewish people's emotions when they read the document that told their death sentence had been changed and that they were to live?

5. What did many of the people of the provinces do according to Esther 8:17?

6 a. It's obvious that God does not want people to accept Christ for such a motive as Esther 8:17 describes. Christians should express attitudes and emotions as described in Esther 8:16. It is this quality of life that will draw others to the Lord Jesus Christ. How does Galatians 5:22,23 describe this quality of life the Holy Spirit wants to channel through every believer in Jesus Christ?

b. (Personal) Have you yielded your life to the Lord Jesus Christ and are you allowing yourself to be a channel of the fruit of the Holy Spirit? Determine which area you need to pray about today (see Phil. 2:13).

FOURTH DAY: Read Esther 9:1-19.

1. What were the Jewish people allowed to do according to Esther 9:2?

2. This chapter is difficult for peace-loving people to read and digest. Today there is still no permanent peace in the world. God promises the day is coming when men will no longer fight. What do these two verses say concerning this wonderful promise of God?

Isaiah 2:4

Micah 4:3

3. God's people were in great danger. There were many foes and they had to fight for their lives. In fact, many of the people of the provinces may not have heard or read the second decree of the king freeing the Jews from their death penalty! Do you believe the

119

Jewish people were morally right to fight for their lives and their families' lives?

4. Read Esther 9:16. What does the last phrase in this verse indicate to you about the purpose of this fighting?

5. Today Christians are instructed in God's Word to live together in joy and unity. Read Psalm 133. Choose key phrases from this Psalm that challenge you to be at peace and in fellowship with all those who have faith in Jesus Christ as their Lord and Savior.

6. **Challenge:** The following verses speak of our bond of fellowship and oneness as Christians. What do they mean to you?

   John 13:34,35

   John 17:11,21

   Romans 12:4,5

   Hebrews 2:11

FIFTH DAY: Read Esther 9:20-32 and Esther 10:1-3.

1. What victorious celebration was instituted and is celebrated to this day by the Jewish people? (see Esther 9:20-22).

120

2. (Personal) Do you have times of remembrance in your life and family? Do you think such days are important? Why? Share, if possible, some ideas with the group.

3. What did Esther and Mordecai call these days of remembrance? Why did they use this word? Give verses.

4. How many years was this celebration to be carried on by the Jewish people?

5 a. According to Esther 10 what kind of leader did Mordecai become, and what words are used to describe him?

   b. (Personal) As you read of Mordecai in Esther 10, what character traits of his would you like to ask God to work out in your life as you make yourself available to him?

6. What verse did you memorize this week to claim as a promise from the Lord?

SIXTH DAY: Read all the Notes and look up the Scriptures.

1. What new thought did you find helpful in the Notes?

2. What personal application did you select to apply to your own life this week?

121

Study Notes

In Esther chapter 7 judgment was pronounced upon Haman and he was hung from the gallows he had made to hang his enemy, Mordecai. However, the decree that had been issued at his request before his death still stood (see Esther 3:7-15). This decree proclaimed that all of the Jews living in King Ahasuerus's 127 provinces, all the way from India to Ethiopia, were to be killed.

An Irreversible Decision Esther 8:1-14

The decree, which ordered this great slaughter of the Jewish race, was impossible to change; even the king could not change it. According to the law of the Medes and the Persians, the king must obey his own law! We have already seen this principle in operation when King Ahasuerus decreed to set aside his first queen, Vashti. Later he probably wanted to take her back, but the decree said that he could not (see Esther 1:18,19,22; 2:1).

When Esther first heard of the decree against her people, she knew the king could not sit down and cancel the previous order that they all be killed. However, she knew that he could send out a new order to permit the Jews to defend themselves. We read of Esther's efforts to undo Haman's evil plot in Esther 5, 6 and 7.

In Esther 8:1,2 the king gave Queen Esther Haman's house and in turn Esther gave to Mordecai all the responsibility that this entailed. This would also include Haman's position of leadership in the land; and as a sign that Mordecai had been given this leadership, the king removed his signet ring, which he had taken from Haman, and gave it to Mordecai (see Esther 8:2).

Man Is Not the Enemy

There is no hint that Esther or Mordecai gloried in the death of Haman, even though he was a wicked man who had plotted the death of their people. It was not the man himself, but what he had planned against their people that made him their enemy. This was no personal feud such as Haman had planned against Mordecai. In fact, Esther had asked nothing of worldly goods for herself, but it was the king, himself, who had initiated giving her Haman's estate. Perhaps the king viewed Haman's action as treason, and in such instances it was traditional that the criminal's possessions were given to the state.

A secondary benefit to all that had happened was that Esther was allowed the freedom to share the fact that Mordecai had adopted her as a child and been both a father and a mother to her through all of these years. As we contrast Esther and Mordecai's honorable actions to Haman's wickedness, we realize that God blesses those who follow in His ways and are obedient in love toward Him. Psalm 1 puts it this way: "Happy the man who never follows the advice of the wicked, or loiters on the way that sinners take, or sits about with scoffers, but finds his pleasure in the law of Yahweh [God], and murmurs his law day and night. He is like a tree that is planted by water streams, yielding its fruit in season, its leaves never fading; success attends all he does. It is nothing like this with the wicked, nothing like this! No, these are like chaff, blown away by the wind. The wicked will not stand firm when Judgment comes, nor sinners when the virtuous assemble. For Yahweh takes care of the way the virtuous go, but the way of the wicked is doomed" (Ps. 1:1-8, *JB*).

Persecution Is Real

It's true that Christian believers may know persecution by unbelievers today. Yet there are many promises in God's Word that are true and need to be claimed by us in such situations. We are not to be surprised when persecution comes our way, nor think it strange nor unusual! In fact, we are to rejoice, because we are being allowed to be a partaker of Christ's sufferings (see 1 Peter 4:12-14). "Blessings are upon the head of the just: but violence covereth the mouth of the wicked" (Prov. 10:6, *KJV*).

> *We are not to be surprised when persecution comes our way, nor think it strange nor unusual! In fact, we are to rejoice, because we are being allowed to be a partaker of Christ's sufferings.*

Do you trust the Lord Jesus Christ in your difficult times? Are you counting upon His promises to see you through, and to honor you at the final judgment, because you have stood firm in your faith in Him as your Savior and Lord? (see 2 Tim. 2:12). "The hope of the righteous shall be gladness: but the expectation of the wicked shall perish. The way of the Lord is strength to the upright: but destruction shall be to the workers of iniquity. The righteous shall never be moved: but the wicked shall not inhabit the earth" (Prov. 10:28-30, KJV).

The Lord Jesus Christ has promised that He shall return to this earth, and He describes the result of His final judgment on man in Isaiah 65:13,14: "Behold, my servants shall rejoice, but ye shall be ashamed: Behold, my servants shall sing for joy of heart, but ye shall cry for sorrow of heart, and shall howl for vexation of spirit" (KJV).

Are You Committed?

There may be some of you who have a question mark in your mind as to whether you have ever committed your life to the Lord Jesus Christ. Many people today say, "I am a Christian; I am on my way to heaven; I belong to Christ." But if they do not do what Christ tells them to do, they are not telling the truth. "If we say that we have no sin, we are only fooling ourselves, and refusing to accept the truth. But if we confess our sins to him, he can be depended on to forgive us and to cleanse us from every wrong. [And it is perfectly proper for God to do this for us because Christ died to wash away our sins.] . . . My little children, I am telling you this so that you will stay away from sin. But if you sin, there is someone to plead for you before the Father. His name is Jesus Christ, the one who is all that is good and who pleases God completely. He is the one who took God's wrath against our sins upon himself, and brought us into fellowship with God; and he is the forgiveness for our sins" (1 John 1:8,9; 2:1,2, TLB).

Will you choose to allow Jesus Christ to cleanse you from your sin, and to use you in a new and exciting way, just as Esther and Mordecai allowed God to use them in their day?

A Queen Makes Her Plea

Mordecai had full right to issue a counter decree in the king's name, which would be just as irreversible as the one issued by Haman. Esther, in tears, kneeling at the king's feet, pled with him to allow Mordecai this favor. As the king had graciously done when she had first sought an audience with him, he used the royal gesture of extending his golden sceptre, a symbol of his authority, toward her to indicate that she had found favor in his sight.

Esther then made her plea for her people who had been ordered to be destroyed. "For how can I endure to see the calamity which shall befall my people, and how can I endure to see the destruction of

124

my kindred?" (Esther 8:6, *NASB*). This takes us back to the statement that Mordecai made to Esther long ago: "And who knows whether you have not come to the kingdom for such a time as this?" (Esther 4:14, *RSV*).

You're in the Kingdom for a Special Reason

If only you could catch a glimpse of the truth in this statement for your life as a Christian! God has brought you into His kingdom at a very special time! If you believe in Jesus Christ as your Lord and Savior, He has a very special purpose for your life, "As the servants of Christ, doing the will of God from the heart; with good will doing service, as to the Lord, and not to men" (Eph. 6:6,7, *KJV*). Think of all those you know who do not know the Lord Jesus Christ as their Savior and Lord, and meditate upon these words, "To do good and to communicate forget not: for with such sacrifices God is well pleased" (Heb. 13:16, *KJV*; see also Jas. 1:22-25; 1 Sam. 12:24).

Who knows whether you have not come to the kingdom for such a time as this? Set up your priorities today! Make a list of those people the Lord lays on your heart. "For how can I endure to see the calamity that is coming to my people? Or how can I endure to see the destruction of my kindred?" (see Esther 8:6).

Remember the words of God found in John 3:17,18. "For God sent not his Son into the world to condemn the world; but that the world through him might be saved. He that believeth on him is not condemned: but he that believeth not is condemned already, because he hath not believed in the name of the only begotten Son of God" (*KJV*). Pray for those on your own personal list. Bring them before God's throne daily in love asking that they may know the only begotten Son, the Lord Jesus Christ.

Perhaps you would like to write the following verse upon a card to carry with you or to place somewhere in your home to remind you to pray for these people whom God has laid upon your heart. "Moreover, as for me, far be it from me that I should sin against the Lord by ceasing to pray for you; but I will instruct you in the good and right way. Only fear the Lord and serve Him in truth with all your heart; for consider what great things He has done for you" (1 Sam. 12:23,24, *NASB*).

In the Name of the King!

The official letters with the new law freeing the Jews from death were now prepared in the same way as those that Haman had sent out (see Esther 3:12-15). The date was June 25, 424 B.C., a little over two months after the first decree was issued. This new law allowed more than eight months for the Jewish people to prepare their defenses against any who might attempt to kill them even after reading the decree (see Esther 8:9).

Scribes and translators were summoned to accomplish this colossal task, for there were 127 provinces with many languages on the mailing list. The palace of Shushan certainly must have boasted an intellectual staff of linguists to have accomplished such a task! The Jews in each part of the empire also had to be notified of the good news.

The writing was in the name of the king and sealed with his ring, and when finished the letters were sent immediately by couriers on horses used in the king's service (see Esther 8:8-10).

Behold, Shouts of Victory! Esther 8:15-17, 9:1-9

The whole city rejoiced and shouted as Mordecai came out from the presence of the king, dressed in royal robes of blue and white, with a great golden crown upon his head. The Jews had "light and gladness and joy and honor" (Esther 8:16, *NASB*). In fact, as the king's edict arrived to every province and city, this same gladness and joy pervaded the Jewish community. They all held feasts and had a holiday. Many of the people of the country declared themselves Jews by faith because of their fear of what the Jews might do to them!

Picture the scene in any one of these little towns where the Jews were dressed in sackcloth and ashes, and felt hopeless because of Haman's edict. Suddenly a rider appears on the horizon and approaches the town bulletin board. Here he nails a notice, quickly mounts his horse and is off to the next small village. Everyone crowds around the bulletin board to see what is there! They are amazed! The king is now on the side of the death-marked people and he urges them to band together and protect themselves. The Jewish people who read the new message cannot believe their eyes! It's too wonderful to be true. Now they are to be spared!

God's People Do Not Seek Revenge

The Jewish people prepared themselves not for vengeance but for self-defense. "The Jews gathered themselves together in their cities throughout all the provinces of King Ahasuerus, to lay hands on such as sought their hurt" (Esther 9:2, *KJV*). These people were not the aggressors; they were defending themselves against those who had prepared to annihilate them. Undoubtedly some Jewish people were killed and certainly some of the enemy were slain on that day.

126

We know that there was no indiscriminate slaughter of masses, but many died on this day of reckoning. About 75,000 people were killed by the Jews. However, it is only fair to point out that this is from a population of 73 million people and we need to realize that this had been the appointed day for the massacre of some 3 million Jews.

It was on March 1, 473 B.C. that the fateful day arrived. The Jews were allowed to gather into compact groups within their various cities to await their attackers (see Esther 9:1-4). All of the rulers of the provinces helped the Jews because of their fear of Mordecai, who had grown more and more powerful throughout the whole kingdom (see Esther 9:3). Here again is evidence of the hand of God, though His name is not mentioned.

There were many Persian citizens who took full advantage of the first decree to attack their hated Jewish neighbors. They had resented in the first place these Jewish people being brought into their land. Deprived of their government support and faced by newly encouraged Jewish people, the Persians were totally defeated (see Esther 9:5-10). In Shushan alone, 500 Persians plus Haman's sons were slain.

It is especially noteworthy to realize that the Jewish people took no advantage of their rightful privilege to take the spoils of those whom they had killed. They took no household goods, money or any other rightful privilege that their culture normally approved of, in order that the purity of their motive—protection of their lives—be made evident to all (see Esther 9:10).

Esther's request for Haman's sons to be hanged seemed out of line with her general character. Yet we must remember that there was no personal vengeance on her part. She was seeking to make a deep impression upon all of the people of Persia, that punishment must fall on those who are responsible for the terrible plot to massacre God's people.

On March 13, 473 B.C., in the capital city of Shushan, the king reported to Queen Esther that 500 men had been slain plus the 10 sons of Haman (see Esther 9:12).

Esther asked the king to let the Jews be allowed one more day to carry out the edict of protecting themselves against those who sought to kill them. Apparently Esther had heard of a Persian plot to attack the Jews on the following day as well, so she asked permission that they be able to defend themselves one more day. The king granted her request and the Jews were allowed one more day to kill their enemies in Shushan. Therefore, on the fourteenth day they also battled in Shushan. Mordecai's letter had specified only one day for the Jews to defend themselves (see Esther 8:13), but Esther's special decree was obeyed also (see Esther 9:15).

Importance of Communication

Note how the survival of the Jewish race and their joy depended on Esther and Mordecai's faithfulness in writing a letter! God uses His people to write letters, telephone or make personal visits today to get out the message of His love and concern for all people. How about you? How responsive are you when God nudges you to write a letter or telephone someone?

Many people fulfill these functions today, helping those who are blind, elderly and crippled. We are also reminded of the Bible translators of our day who perform a similar service as all of the scribes who wrote the letters in different languages to the provinces. Today we have many dedicated people, located in the jungles of the world, among the different tribes translating the Bible and teaching people to read, in order that they too might hear of God's love for them in sending His only Son, the Lord Jesus Christ, to be their Savior and Lord.

The kind of love God wants to channel through your life is the kind that can cause you to care for an enemy, and take the lead to love without any cause.

What about you? Do you believe that God might call you to be of some similar service? Perhaps He may call you to be a letter-writer, a communicator in some way, or even a missionary to go to some far off place to translate the Bible for people who have never heard the Good News about the Lord Jesus Christ. Are you willing to pray today and ask God what He would have you do with your life concerning such matters?

Love Shows in Our Deeds

Love is commanded over 25 times in the New Testament. Since love is commanded, it needs to be expressed deliberately and consciously by Christians. The proof of love is not in words, but in deeds. Even Christ's love had to pass this test. In John 14:31 Christ said, "But that the world may know that I love the Father; and as the Father gave me commandment, even so I do" (*KJV*). Our obedience to the Lord Jesus Christ will show that we love Him.

As you read through the pages of the Bible, stop at every command to love, and ask yourself, "Is this true of me or isn't it?" It's not just looking inside to see if you have a nice, warm feeling that tells you if you love the Lord. No, it must be a calm, deliberate checking of yourself against God's commands to see if you are willing to obey them. And when you do, your heart is flooded with joy and peace and a sense of God's presence.

"Uncle Cam" (W.C. Townsend—the Wycliffe Bible Translators' founder) told how God called him to go to the USSR. He argued with God for two days saying, "Lord, I'm seventy years old. I'm not the one to go. Latin America is my place; that's where I feel at home." He argued and argued with the Lord, and said that he was the most miserable Christian he had ever known for those two days. It was absolute agony. He had never known such torture, such agony of spirit, such loss of joy, such confusion of mind, until he finally said, "I will;" at that moment the Lord flooded his heart with joy and blessing and peace. His obedience brought the feeling of a right relationship with God. (From the Wycliffe Bible Translators publication—May 1975.)

An Initiating Kind of Love

This kind of love is expected of us. It is an initiating kind of love, not just a responding kind of love. You are not to wait for someone else to love that person and do something for that person's benefit. Whether or not this love will bring you any benefit doesn't matter. The kind of love God wants to channel through your life is the kind that can cause you to care for an enemy, and take the lead to love without any cause.

It is the Holy Spirit that can produce this kind of love in you, plus the other fruit God has promised in Galatians 5:22,23. God wants to give us the mind and commitment that we will be obedient to act in the benefit of others, regardless of how they act toward us! And we are not to try to do it ourselves. Our attitude should be one of knowing that "It is God who is at work in you, both to will and to work for His good pleasure" (Phil. 2:13, *NASB*). Will you show your love for God this week by deliberately setting yourself up to be obedient to work for His glory, as He guides you?

God's People Are Called to Celebrate!
Esther 9:20-32 and 10

After God's marvelous deliverance, we find that a feast is instituted by Mordecai called the Feast of Purim. Mordecai wrote out the details and sent letters to all the Jews that were in the provinces of King Ahasuerus. The people were to keep the fourteenth and fifteenth days of the month of Adar and celebrate it as the days when the Jews rested from their enemies, a time when their sorrow was

129

turned to joy and their mourning into a good day. It was to be a day of feasting, joy, of sending portions to one another and gifts to the poor. Each generation was to be responsible to tell the story to the one following. This has been marvelously carried out into our own times some 2500 years later. Orthodox Jewish people around the world keep the Feast of Purim.

Today the first evening of the Feast of Purim is commemorated by the Orthodox Jews in their synagogues. It is a celebration of gladness and is concluded by the reading of the book of Esther. As they read it the people spit as the name of Haman is mentioned. They are also allowed to use such expressions as, "Let his name be blotted out," or "Let him be accursed." The following day they come together for a joyful service, for it is a feast that celebrates their deliverance by God. They also include subsequent deliverances such as that from the German-Nazi atrocities.

Now where was Queen Esther and what was she doing during the crisis days? Had it been announced that she was of the Jewish race? The record is silent on these questions. We can only ponder and believe that she looked back over the ways God had kept her and thanked Him for taking her as an obscure captive and placing her on the throne beside the great emperor "for such a time as this."

God Is Still on His Throne

As we think of these people marking the day of their deliverance and celebrating God's goodness to them down though the generations and up to today, it should be a reminder first of all of the sovereignty of God. Today God is on the throne just as He was in Esther's day. All nations, people and lands are under His control. He controls His entire universe and all of the forces of nature.

Another thought we can arrive at as we study the book of Esther, is that God takes many years to prepare His servants for a period of service. God had watched over Esther through the loss of her family and her trip to Persia. He watched over her through her adoption by Mordecai.

If you feel right now that you are not in a place where God is using you, remember that He may be preparing you for some vital service at a later time. It is not up to us to choose our path, nor to estimate our usefulness to God in any situation. Remember that God never wastes anything, and certainly not the lives of His children. He designates our service and our geographical location. We never know when our greatest hour will be.

Winston Churchill said during the Battle of Britain in 1941, "We have the honor to stand alone! Let us so conduct ourselves in these days of crisis that when future historians write the story of our people they will say, 'This was their finest hour.'" Will you trust God to write your story this way?

God's Wonderful Timing

We have also learned from the book of Esther about God's wonderful timing. God has no limitation and is always able to rescue us just in time. This was powerfully demonstrated when Haman chose the day for the Jews to be slain, and then God chose the day for them to be saved. Isn't it a comfort to know that God is not only the Master Designer of this world, but also the Master of its every detail?

God, who directed the life of Esther and Mordecai, is the God who wants to direct your life, too. The God and Father of our Lord Jesus Christ loves us with an everlasting love and is waiting for us to come to Him each day in faith and obedience. Joyfully give all that you have in service to Him until that day when you will see Him face to face.

King Ahasuerus died in 465 B.C. His reign as king was one of power and wealth. Again we see the marvelous providence of God as He elevated a despised Jew to a position of honor in such an empire. Just as God took notice of Mordecai and used him, God is aware of what we are doing and how we are doing it for Him. "For God is not unrighteous to forget your work and labour of love, which ye have shewed toward his name" (Heb. 6:10, KJV).

Each of us has opportunities to be used by God. Have you been asked to be a Sunday School teacher, to sing in the choir; has God asked you to show concern for a neighbor or business associate? There are times when God asks you to put the welfare of other people before your own personal comfort and pleasure. Mordecai and Esther served their generation. Are you willing by the power of the Holy Spirit to serve your generation?